Pecan Lovers' Cook Book

by Mark Blazek

Golden West Publishers

Cover design and artwork by Bruce Robert Fischer

Library of Congress Cataloging-in-Publication Data

Blazek, Mark
    Pecan lovers' cook book.

    Includes index.
    1. Cookery (Pecans)   I. Title.
TX814.2.P4B57   1986   641.6'452   86–25812
ISBN 0–914846–27–2

Printed in the United States of America

Information in this book is deemed to be authentic and accurate by author and publisher. However, they disclaim any liability incurred in connection with the use of information appearing in this book.

Golden West Publishers
4113 N. Longview Ave.
Phoenix, AZ 85014. USA

Dedication

Thank you, Mom.

This one's for you!

Foreword

When I was living and attending school in the small town of Socorro, New Mexico (population: 5000), I'd make occasional pilgrimages to the southern part of the state to pick up shelled pecans from the farms in the Rio Grande Valley for $1.99 per pound (unshelled nuts were 99¢ per pound). I'd always try to ship or take some home for my mom in Chicago who shared my delight in the nut.

Both of us burned quite a few nuts before we finally figured out how to make quality spiced pecans. From that point some six or seven years ago, I began collecting and creating pecan-related recipes, the result of which you now hold in your hands.

Presently, I am living in Austin, Texas, where, in season, you can collect fallen pecans off the streets and sidewalks in unlimited quantities. If I could remember all of those who contributed information (and their taste buds!) to this collection, I'd send each a bushel basket of pecans in appreciation. You all know who you are. You are my friends.

Mark C. Blazek

Contents

About Pecans
for Your Information ...

● The pecan is the most popular nut tree native to the United States. It is a species of hickory (*Carya illinoensis*) and belongs to the same plant family as walnuts.

● Pecan trees prefer a rich, deep, well-drained soil and long, warm growing seasons. They grow naturally in Mexico and northeastward through central and eastern Texas, Louisiana, Mississippi, Alabama, Arkansas, central and eastern Oklahoma, eastern Kansas, western Illinois and southeastern Iowa. Under cultivation, pecans grow also in New Mexico, Arizona, California, Florida, Georgia, and North and South Carolina.

● The pecan has not proved commercially successful north of latitude 40 degrees. Although trees will survive in much of the Northwest and Northeast, the cooler summers don't allow development of full kernels. Thus, a number of southeastern states (Texas, Oklahoma, Louisiana, Mississippi, Georgia and Florida) and California furnish the bulk of the commercial crop. Georgia is by far the leading producer of the nut.

● There are more than 35 pecan varieties. They differ in relative production, kernel quality and disease resistance. Most nuts have a rounded oblong shape and vary in weight from 25 to 100 to the pound. The varieties called "paper shells" are considered most desirable.

● The pecan tree is deciduous and is capable of attaining 150 feet in height. Some pecan tree trunks measure seven feet thick. In the southeastern United States the pecan is called the "tax tree" because a few trees planted around the house will provide extra income during the fall—and help pay county property taxes!

● Pecans rate behind peanuts and pinon nuts in proportion of shell to edible meat. The edible portion of the pecan nut is 56.4 percent, compared with 75.5 percent for peanuts and 58.1 percent for pinon nuts. Average United States consumption of pecans is eight ounces per person.

APPETIZERS

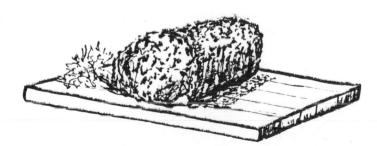

South-of-the-Border Cheese Ball

1 lb. MONTEREY JACK CHEESE (shredded)
1 pkg. (8 oz.) CREAM CHEESE
½ cup JALAPEÑO PEPPERS (finely-chopped)
dash SALT
GARLIC CLOVES (minced) (optional)
1 cup PECANS (finely chopped)

Soften cheeses. Add jalapeño and salt (and garlic, if desired), and mix until smooth. Chill mixture in refrigerator until firm enough to shape into a ball. Roll ball in chopped pecans and chill until serving time.

All of the cheese balls mentioned here may be rolled into logs if desired. They may also be frozen and stored for later use.

Roasted Pecans

1 cup PECAN HALVES
4 Tbsp. (½ stick) BUTTER
SALT

Preheat oven to 300 degrees. Melt butter in a saucepan. Pour melted butter on a cookie sheet. Add pecan halves. Stir pecan halves in the butter, coating them on both sides. Bake on one side about 10 minutes, lightly salt to taste, turn the halves over, add more salt (if desired), and bake 10 more minutes.

Honey-Glazed Pecans

1 cup SUGAR
2 Tbsp. HONEY
½ cup MILK
¾ tsp. VANILLA EXTRACT
SALT to taste
2 cups PECAN HALVES*

Combine all ingredients except pecans. Cook in saucepan to 240 degrees. Add pecans and stir. Continue cooking for one minute. Pour on waxed-paper-lined cookie sheet and separate with forks into individual nuts or desired clumps. Cool.

*You can use pecan halves or pecan pieces here. If you use pieces, you may wish to let the nuts cool in small clusters of nuts.

For variation, try substituting ¾ tsp. of mint extract for the vanilla. Or, instead of milk and vanilla, try ½ cup of orange juice and 1 tsp. of grated orange rind.

Purists may substitute ½ cup of water and ½ tsp. nutmeg, cloves, or cinnamon for the milk and vanilla.

Nutty Pineapple-Cheese Ball

2 pkgs. (8 oz. each) CREAM CHEESE
1 can (8 oz.) crushed PINEAPPLE (well-drained)
2 cups PECANS (chopped)
1/3 cup BELL PEPPER (chopped)
2 Tbsp. GREEN ONION (chopped)
1 Tbsp. SEASONED SALT
GARNISH (optional)

Soften cream cheese. Gradually stir in crushed pineapple, one cup pecans, bell pepper, onion and seasoned salt. Chill well. Form into a ball and roll in one cup pecans. Chill until serving. Garnish with twists of pineapple slices, maraschino cherries, or parsley. Serve with assorted crackers.

Curried Nut Combo

2 cups ALMONDS (shelled)
2 cups WALNUTS (shelled)
2 cups PECANS (shelled)
½ cup OLIVE OIL
1 tsp. TABASCO SAUCE
1 tsp. WORCESTERSHIRE SAUCE
1 Tbsp. CURRY

Combine all ingredients and mix well. Spread mixture on a greased cookie sheet. Separate individual nuts from each other. Bake in a 325 degree oven until lightly toasted (about 10-14 minutes). Let cool on paper towels and season to taste with salt.

Cheesey Snack Ball

1 jar (5 oz.) BLUE CHEESE SPREAD
1 jar (5 oz.) SHARP CHEDDAR CHEESE SPREAD
1 pkg. (8 oz.) CREAM CHEESE
1 pkg. (8 oz.) SHARP CHEDDAR CHEESE
3 Tbsp. WINE VINEGAR
2 cloves GARLIC (minced)
½ cup PECANS (finely-chopped)

Soften cheese. Blend all ingredients, except nuts, until smooth. Chill mixture in refrigerator until firm enough to shape into a ball. Roll ball in chopped pecans and chill until serving time.

Garlic lovers may wish to increase the amount of garlic, but please do not use anything other than fresh garlic cloves (no dehydrated material).

For another interesting variation, try adding a 3-oz. pkg. of finely-chopped, pressed and cooked beef.

Devil's Log O' Nuts

8 oz. CREAM CHEESE (softened)
12 oz. SHARP CHEDDAR CHEESE (grated fine)
1 cup PECANS (chopped fine)
4 Tbsp. CHILI POWDER

Combine cream cheese, cheddar cheese and nuts. Mix well. Form into a log and refrigerate for at least one hour. Remove from refrigerator and roll in chili powder until outside surface is entirely coated. Roll log in wax paper or plastic wrap and refrigerate until ready to use. Serve with crackers.

Cinnamon Pecan Bites

2 cups SUGAR
¼ tsp. CREAM OF TARTAR
1½ tsp. CINNAMON
½ cup WATER
2 tsp. LIGHT CORN SYRUP
3 cups PECANS (halves preferred)

Combine all ingredients except nuts. Cook to a firm ball stage (246 degrees F.)* Add nuts and stir until coated. Spread on waxed paper to cool. Using two forks, separate each nut.

*It is important to heat the mixture to at least 246 degrees. Use a candy thermometer, or test for firm ball stage.

Deviled Pecans

1 lb. SHELLED PECANS
1/3 cup of melted BUTTER
1 Tbsp. WORCESTERSHIRE SAUCE
½ tsp. TABASCO SAUCE
¼ tsp. PEPPER
1 tsp. SALT

Preheat oven to 300 degrees. Place nuts in shallow baking pan. Combine remaining ingredients. Pour over nuts and stir well. Bake 20 minutes, stirring twice during the cooking. Let cool on thick paper towels. Store in airtight container.

Honey-Roasted Pecans

3 cups PECAN HALVES
3 Tbsp. HONEY
2 Tbsp. APPLE CIDER VINEGAR
4 Tbsp. BUTTER (melted)
SALT

1. Place honey and vinegar into a large jar with a tight-fitting lid. Fill jar with pecans to about one-half inch of top. Shake jar well until all the nuts are well-coated with honey/vinegar mixture.
2. Spread nuts on cookie sheet. Separate the nuts with two forks. Place cookie sheet under medium-high broiler for about 5 minutes. CAUTION: You must watch nuts constantly to make certain they do not burn.
3. Remove the cookie sheet from the oven and turn heat down to 300 degrees. Brush nuts with melted butter. Return the nuts to the oven and bake at 300 degrees for about 20 minutes. Shake pan every 5 minutes to keep nuts from sticking and to help them roast evenly. Remove from oven and sprinkle with salt to taste. Cool and store in air-tight container.*

*WARNING: Do not freeze these nuts as the coating becomes messy after thawing.

Recipe Notes

_____

_____

_____

_____

_____

_____

_____

_____

_____

_____

_____

_____

_____

_____

_____

_____

_____

_____

_____

_____

_____

_____

SALADS

Mom's Sweet and Fruity Pecan Salad*

1 can (21 oz.) CHERRY PIE FILLING
1 can (20 oz.) CRUSHED PINEAPPLE
1 can (14 oz.) SWEETENED CONDENSED MILK
1 container (8 or 9 oz.) WHIPPED TOPPING
    (thawed)
½ cup PECANS (chopped)

Drain pineapple well. Mix all ingredients together well. Chill for at least 4 hours and, preferably, overnight.

*Nearly every Christmas, Mom sends me one of the new recipes she has tried. This is her Christmas 1984 discovery—simple, quick and delicious!

All-Purpose Pecan Salad Dressing

1 pkg. (3 oz.) CREAM CHEESE
1/3 cup MAYONNAISE
1/3 cup ORANGE JUICE
1 Tbsp. LEMON JUICE
1 Tbsp. SUGAR
¼ tsp. SALT
1/3 cup PECANS (chopped)

Soften cream cheese. Add remaining ingredients except pecans. Beat until well blended. Stir in pecans. Chill well. Serve with fruit or crisp salad greens. Yields 1 1/3 cups.

Nutty Turkey & Blue Cheese Salad

Salad:
4 cups LETTUCE of your choice (torn)
2 cups fresh SPINACH (torn)
1 cup fresh MUSHROOMS (sliced)
2 cups COOKED TURKEY (diced)
1 cup RED ONION RINGS

Combine salad ingredients. Cover and chill.

Dressing:
1 container (8 oz.) PLAIN YOGURT
½ cup PECANS (chopped)
1/3 cup BLUE CHEESE (crumbled)
1 tsp. SUGAR
½ tsp. SALT
½ tsp. CELERY SEED
¼ tsp. BASIL

Combine yogurt, nuts, blue cheese, sugar, salt, celery seed and basil. Mix well. Pour dressing over greens and toss to serve.

Simple Springtime Salad*

2 pkgs. (3 oz. each) LEMON GELATIN
1 pkg. (8 oz.) CREAM CHEESE
1½ cups PECANS (chopped)
1 can (15¼-oz.) CRUSHED PINEAPPLE

Chill gelatin until slightly firm. Mix other three ingredients, blending well. Stir into gelatin and mold. Serve on a bed of lettuce.

*Use this recipe as a base to which you may add your favorite other nuts and chopped vegetables and fruits.

Black Cherry & Olive Salad

3½ cups BING CHERRIES (pitted)
1/3 cup LEMON JUICE
1 pkg. (3 oz.) ORANGE GELATIN
¾ cup PECANS (chopped)
1 bottle (3 oz.) STUFFED OLIVES (sliced)

Drain cherries; add water to cherry syrup and lemon juice to make 1¾ cups liquid. Heat; pour over gelatin and stir until dissolved. Chill until partially set. Add cherries, pecans and olives. Pour into individual molds or shallow pan; chill until firm. Serve on lettuce with mayonnaise.

Mark's Macaroni Mess

1 lb. ELBOW MACARONI
½ cup VINEGAR
½ cup SALAD OIL
¼ tsp. PAPRIKA
SALT and PEPPER (to taste)
¾ cup PECANS (chopped)
1 cup HAM (cut in strips)
1 cup AMERICAN CHEESE (cut in strips)
¾ cup GREEN PEPPER (chopped)
¼ cup SCALLIONS (sliced)

Cook macaroni in boiling salted water until tender. Drain and rinse with cold water. In a large bowl, combine vinegar, oil, salt and pepper. Add macaroni and remaining ingredients. Toss lightly. Cover and chill at least one hour before serving. Makes 8-10 servings.

Stuffed Date & Fruit Salad

6 large PEACH HALVES
6 LETTUCE CUPS
6 whole FIGS (canned)
12 APRICOT HALVES
6 DATES (pitted)
¼ cup PECANS (finely-chopped)

Arrange peach halves, cut side up, on crisp lettuce. Top with a fig and 2 apricot halves. Stuff dates with nuts, place one on each salad. Makes 6 servings.

Stuffed Cinnamon Apple Salad

6 APPLES
½ cup RED CINNAMON CANDIES
¼ cup SUGAR
2 cups WATER
½ cup broken PECAN pieces
10 DATES (pitted and chopped)
½ cup PINEAPPLE (diced)
¼ cup SALAD DRESSING

Pare and core apples. Cook candies and sugar in water until dissolved; add whole apples and cook slowly until transparent but not soft. Chill. Combine remaining ingredients; stuff apples with this mixture and serve on lettuce. Sprinkle with ground cinnamon, if desired.

Nutty-Crunchy Orange Salad

1 large ORANGE (seedless)
LETTUCE
1 cup APPLES (pared and diced)
1 cup CELERY (diced)
½ cup PECANS (chopped)
SALT (to taste)
4 Tbsp. MAYONNAISE

Pare orange, cut into 5 slices and place in lettuce cups on individual plates. Combine other ingredients, tossing lightly together, and pile in light heaps on orange slices. Serve at once.

Thanksgiving Pecan Salad

1 can (15¼ oz.) PINEAPPLE CHUNKS
2 pkgs. (3 oz. each) CHERRY GELATIN
1 can (16 oz.) WHOLE CRANBERRY SAUCE
1 cup COLD WATER
1 cup CELERY (chopped)
½ cup PECANS (chopped)

Drain pineapple, reserve syrup. Add enough water to syrup to make one cup liquid. Bring to a boil and dissolve gelatin in hot liquid. Add one cup cold water. Chill until thick but not set. Stir in cranberry sauce, pineapple, celery and pecans. Pour into 2-quart mold. Chill until firm. Unmold.

*Ambrosia Fruit Dip

1 container (8 oz.) FRUIT YOGURT (any flavor)
½ cup FLAKED COCONUT
½ cup CREAM OF COCONUT
¼ cup PECANS (toasted and chopped)

In a small bowl, combine yogurt, coconut and cream of coconut. Mix well and stir in pecans. Refrigerate for at least 2 hours before serving with fresh fruit. (Or toss with 8 to 10 cups of cut-up assorted fresh fruit for a special fruit salad.)

*From a Greek word meaning "immortal," mythological ambrosia was the food of the gods and other immortals.

Crunchy Pineapple & Cream Salad

1 large can (15-20 oz.) CRUSHED PINEAPPLE
1 pkg. (3 oz.) LIME GELATIN
1 cup CARROTS (grated)
1 cup CELERY (diced)
1 cup PECANS (chopped)
1 cup EVAPORATED MILK (chilled)

Simmer gelatin and crushed pineapple together until gelatin dissolves completely. Pour into large mixing bowl and let cool. Stir in carrots, celery and pecans. Whip chilled evaporated milk until thick and fold into gelatin mixture. Place in salad mold and let stand in refrigerator until firm.

Easy Banana-Nut Treats

3 BANANAS (ripe)
¼ cup ORANGE JUICE
½ cup PECANS (finely-chopped)

Peel bananas, cut lengthwise in half and then crosswise in half. To prevent them from discoloring, prepare salads just before serving, and coat bananas at once with orange juice. Roll in chopped nuts, pressing slightly to imbed them. Arrange on lettuce and serve with Pecan Salad Dressing (see recipe) or other preferred dressing.

George Washington Salad

1 pkg. (3 oz.) GELATIN (rasberry or cherry)
1 cup BING CHERRIES (pitted)
1 cup CRUSHED PINEAPPLE (drained)
½ cup PECANS (chopped)
¼ cup SUGAR
Dash of SALT
1 cup BOILING WATER
1 cup COLD WATER

Dissolve gelatin in boiling water; add cold water and chill until partially set. Stir in remaining ingredients. Chill in a mold and serve with mayonnaise on lettuce.

Recipe Notes

_____

_____

_____

_____

_____

_____

_____

_____

_____

_____

_____

_____

_____

_____

_____

_____

_____

_____

_____

_____

_____

_____

MAIN DISHES

Pecan Chicken Casserole

1 cup COOKED CHICKEN (diced)
1 can CREAM OF CHICKEN SOUP (10¾ oz.)
1 cup CELERY (chopped)
2 Tbsp. ONION (chopped)
½ cup PECANS (chopped)
1½ cups COOKED RICE
½ tsp. SALT
¼ tsp. PEPPER
1 Tbsp. LEMON JUICE
½ cup MAYONNAISE
¼ cup WATER
3 EGGS (hard cooked)

Combine chicken, soup, vegetables, nuts and seasoning; blend well. Stir in lemon juice, mayonnaise, water. Chop 2 eggs; add to mixture. Place in greased casserole. Bake at 400 degrees for 15 minutes or until bubbly. Let stand 15 minutes before serving. Garnish with remaining sliced egg. Yields 4 servings.

Creamed Onion Casserole

2 lbs. small WHITE ONIONS
1 can (10¾ oz.) CREAM OF MUSHROOM SOUP
¼ cup MILK
½ cup PECANS (chopped)
SALT and PEPPER
½ cup SHARP CHEDDAR CHEESE (grated)

Cook onions slowly in salted water until almost tender but firm (not more than 10-15 minutes). Drain and put in greased casserole. Mix soup, milk and nuts; season to taste and pour over onions. Top with cheese and bake at 350 degrees about 30 minutes, or until well browned. Yields 6 servings.

Stir-Fried Scallops with Peppers*

SAUCE:
  1 lg. AVOCADO
  1 tsp. LEMON JUICE
  2 tsp. MAYONNAISE or salad dressing
  1 hard-cooked EGG (finely-chopped)
  ¼ tsp. SALT
  ¼ tsp. CAYENNE PEPPER
  1 cup PECANS (finely-chopped)

Mix avocado meat with lemon juice and blend until smooth and creamy. Blend in mayonnaise, egg, salt and pepper. Stir in pecans and set aside.

SCALLOPS/PEPPERS:
  1 stick BUTTER (8 Tbsp.)
  1 Tbsp. OLIVE OIL
  2 green BELL PEPPERS (seeded and thinly-sliced)
  2 red BELL PEPPERS (seeded and thinly-sliced)
  2 cloves GARLIC (finely-chopped)
  1 cup thickly-sliced fresh MUSHROOMS
    (about 4 oz.)
  3 Tbsp. LEMON JUICE
  2 lbs. sea SCALLOPS

1) Heat one-half of butter (4 Tbsp.) and olive oil in a large heavy skillet. Add pepper slices and saute, stirring often, until tender. Arrange pepper slices on a heated serving platter.

2) Add remaining butter and garlic to butter/olive oil leftover in skillet used to prepare the peppers. Cook at medium-heat. Add mushrooms and cook until tender.

3) Mix lemon juice into scallops and stir into butter and mushroom mixture. Cook and stir until scallops are opaque (about 3 to 5 minutes)

4) Serve scallops immediately over peppers. Pass avocado sauce at the table or provide individual portions.

*This recipe makes about 4 servings. The scallops provide a wonderful low-fat source of protein. As an added flair, you may wish to add two Tbsp. of dry sherry to your scallops just after cooking and before serving.

Magnificent Meatballs

2 lbs. GROUND BEEF (the leanest you can afford)
½ cup ONION (finely-chopped)
1 clove GARLIC (minced)
½ cup CORN FLAKES (crushed)
1 tsp. SALT
1 cup MILK
½ cup PECANS (finely-chopped)
2 Tbsp. VEGETABLE OIL
½ cup ONION (finely-chopped)
1½ tsp. CURRY POWDER
1 Tbsp. FLOUR
½ tsp. SALT
1½ cups APPLE JUICE
¼ cup flaked COCONUT

1) Blend meat, ½ cup onion, garlic, corn flakes, one teaspoon salt, milk and pecans together. Shape into about 60 balls (slightly smaller than golf balls). Set aside.

2) Heat oil in a large skillet. Add meatballs. Brown well on all sides and remove from skillet. Drain off all but one Tbsp. of the pan drippings. Add remaining onion. Cook until tender. Stir in curry powder, flour, remaining salt, and apple juice. Mix until well-blended. Cook, stirring constantly, until thick and smooth. Return meatballs to gravy. Cover. Simmer for 5 minutes. Serve topped with coconut.

Orange-Pecan Honeyed Chicken

3 whole unskinned CHICKEN BREASTS (split)
2 Tbsp. BUTTER
¾ cup fresh ORANGE JUICE with pulp
4 Tbsp. HONEY
2 Tbsp. ONION (chopped)
¼ tsp. BLACK PEPPER
SALT
cooked RICE (or wild rice)

1) In a large skillet, brown chicken (skin side down first) in butter on both sides. Add orange juice, honey, onion and black pepper. Season to taste with salt.

2) Cover loosely and simmer for 20-30 minutes, or until chicken is tender.

3) Remove chicken from pan and arrange over your favorite rice mixture. Keep warm. Reserve drippings.

SAUCE:

3 Tbsp. WHITE WINE (or water)
1 Tbsp. FLOUR
1 tsp. ORANGE PEEL (grated)
2 large ORANGES (peeled and sectioned)
½ cup PECANS (finely-chopped)

Stir wine into flour and blend well. Add to reserved pan drippings and cook, stirring constantly until thickened. Add orange peel and sections. Heat thoroughly. Immediately serve over chicken and rice. Makes about 6 servings.

Buttered Zucchini Sticks

1½ cups ZUCCHINI (shredded)
  (about 2 small zucchini)
2 cups sifted FLOUR
3 tsp. BAKING POWDER
1 tsp. SALT
¼ tsp. BAKING SODA
½ tsp. crushed BASIL
½ cup PECANS (finely-chopped)
½ cup SOUR CREAM
1 EGG
6 tsp. BUTTER (melted)

1) Spread zucchini evenly between two layers of paper towels, each layer being several thicknesses of paper towel. Pat gently or lay several magazines on the top layer of towels to soak up excess moisture from zucchini.

2) Stir flour, baking powder, salt and baking soda together. Add basil, pecans and zucchini. Mix well with a fork.

3) Mix sour cream, egg and 2 Tbsp. melted butter together. Add to flour mixture. Stir lightly with fork until liquid is absorbed. Turn onto lightly-floured surface.

4) Pat dough into 8-inch square. Cut square in half. Cut each half crosswise into 6 strips. Roll strips into remaining melted butter. Arrange on a cookie sheet. Bake at 425 degrees for 35 minutes or until golden brown. Cool slightly before serving.

Salmon Casserole with Pecans*

1 box (8 oz.) ELBOW MACARONI (or other pasta)
2 cans (about 7-8 oz. each) SALMON
1 small can PIMENTO
1 small ONION (chopped)
1 cup canned PEAS
4 oz. fresh MUSHROOMS (sliced)
½ cup PECANS (finely-chopped)
2 Tbsp. BUTTER
½ cup MILK
1 can (10¼ oz.) CREAM OF MUSHROOM SOUP
1 tsp. WORCESTERSHIRE SAUCE
1 tsp. SALT
¼ tsp. GROUND PEPPER (fresh-ground
    pepper, if available)

1) Cook macaroni in salted, boiling water, as per directions on package.

2) Drain salmon well and break into pieces. Drain pimento and chop into small pieces. Chop onion fine. Drain peas.

3) Gently mix salmon with peas, pimento, mushrooms and pecans.

4) Melt butter over low flame, add onions and cook until tender but not brown.

5) Add the milk to soup and bring to a boil. Add onions, Worcestershire sauce, salt and pepper. Remove from heat.

6) Mix all ingredients together slowly into a greased casserole dish. Bake in 350 degree oven for about 20 to 30 minutes. Crush potato chips on top before serving, if desired.

*Tip: Salmon is expensive. For a much less expensive alternative, try canned mackerel. If you rinse the mackerel very well while breaking up in cold water, few people will be able to tell you've made this substitution!

Mark's Quick Two-Man Pizza Extravaganza

2 cups BISQUICK (or similar baking mix)
1 cup WATER
1 can TOMATO SOUP
2 tsp. ITALIAN SEASONING (marjoram, thyme, rosemary, savory, sage, oregano and basil combo)*
1 small can CRUSHED PINEAPPLE
4 oz. MUSHROOMS (thinly-sliced) (optional)
4 oz. PEPPERONI (thinly-sliced)
1/3 cup PECANS (finely-chopped)
4 oz. MONTEREY JACK CHEESE (shredded)

1) Combine baking mix with water. Mix well and set aside for five minutes. Then pat into slightly-greased 7x11x1½-inch (or similar) pan.

2) Spread tomato soup in thick layer over dough. Sprinkle Italian seasoning evenly over sauce.

3) Drain crushed pineapple and spread evenly over sauce and herbs after mixing in finely-chopped pecans. Add mushrooms, if desired.

4) Place pepperoni slices neatly over pizza and top with shredded cheese. Sprinkle cheese once again with Italian seasoning, if desired, or try oregano.

5) Place in 300 degree oven for 20 to 30 minutes or until cheese has melted and is golden brown. Remove and serve immediately.

*You may wish to experiment with different toppings and varieties of cheese to suit personal tastes. I've found strong spices undesirable in this recipe. Additionally, though Monterey Jack cheese does not provide the stringiness that mozzarella cheese does, the Monterey Jack does add a more cheesy flavor. This recipe is perfect for two people with hearty appetites. If you use the suggested pan size, you can serve two simple and giant slices!

Stuffed Tomatoes with Bacon*

4 lg. TOMATOES (about 2 lbs.)
8 oz. lean BACON
1 Tbsp. VEGETABLE OIL
½ cup ONION (finely-chopped)
1 clove GARLIC (crushed)
¼ cup PECANS (chopped)
½ cup ZUCCHINI (diced)
½ cup GREEN PEPPER (in ¼-inch squares)
¼ tsp. SALT
1 tsp. BASIL LEAVES (crushed)
⅛ tsp. ground BLACK PEPPER

1) Keep tomatoes at room temperature until fully ripe.

2) Preheat oven to 350 degrees. Cut off stem of each tomato and scoop out and reserve pulp, leaving ¼-inch thick shells. Turn tomatoes open end down to drain.

3) Cut reserved pulp into ¼-inch pieces (yielding about 1½ cups).

4) Heat bacon in small saucepan until cooked but not crisp. Remove bacon, reserving grease. Add vegetable oil, onion and garlic. Saute until onion is transparent (about 5 minutes). Add zucchini, green pepper, salt, basil, black pepper and reserved diced tomato. Cook and stir over medium heat until vegetables are tender (about 4 minutes). Add pecans and bacon; stir gently to mix.

5) Drain off liquid. Spoon vegetable/bacon mixture into tomato shells. Place in a shallow baking pan containing ½-inch of water. Cover and bake until tomatoes are tender (20 to 25 minutes). Makes about 4 portions.

*This is an excellent vegetarian dish—simply leave out the bacon!

Pecan-Barley Casserole

4 Tbsp. VEGETABLE OIL
2 cups GREEN ONIONS (chopped)
½ cup GREEN ONION TOPS (chopped)
¼ cup GREEN PEPPER (chopped)
1/3 cup CELERY (chopped)
1 cup PEARL BARLEY
½ cup cooked CARROTS (diced)
½ cup PECANS (chopped)
5 cups VEGETABLE STOCK
1 tsp. SESAME SALT
½ clove GARLIC (minced)
½ tsp. MARJORAM
½ tsp. BASIL

1) Heat vegetable oil in a skillet and saute onions, green pepper and celery until vegetables are slightly cooked. Remove from pan. Saute barley in same pan until it turns golden brown (about 5 minutes).

2) Combine onions, green pepper, celery and barley with carrots and pecans in a casserole dish. Pour in 2 cups of the vegetable stock. Season with sesame salt, garlic, marjoram and basil. Cover and bake at 350 degrees for 30 minutes.

3) Stir in 2 more cups of stock. Cover and bake another 30 minutes. Add the final cup of stock, mixing well, and bake in a casserole (uncovered) for 15 minutes longer.

Nutty Chicken Crepes

CREPES:
¾ cup FLOUR (sifted)
½ tsp. SALT
1 tsp. BAKING POWDER
2 EGGS (well-beaten)
2/3 cup MILK
1/3 cup WATER
½ tsp. LEMON RIND (grated)

1) Mix dry ingredients. Add eggs, milk, water and lemon rind. Stir only enough to combine ingredients.

2) Lightly grease a skillet and heat to moderate temperature. Pour thin layer of crepe mixture into skillet (or use a crepe maker). Brown lightly on each side and remove. Set aside.

FILLING:
¼ cup BUTTER
3 cubes CHICKEN BOUILLON
¼ cup FLOUR
¼ tsp. POULTRY SEASONING
2 cups MILK
2 cups COOKED CHICKEN (chopped)
1 Tbsp. LEMON JUICE
½ cup CELERY (chopped)
½ cup PECANS (pieces)

1) Heat butter. Add bouillon cubes and mash to dissolve.

2) Blend flour and seasoning together. Add milk, chicken and lemon juice. Cook over low heat until thick. Stir in butter mixture.

3) Fill crepes with chicken filling. Roll up. Mix celery and pecans together and sprinkle over crepes before serving. Makes 8-12 filled crepes.

End-Of-Summer Chicken Casserole

1 lb. CHICKEN BREASTS
8 oz. ELBOW MACARONI
1 pkg. (8 oz.) CREAM CHEESE
1 can SWEET PEAS
½ CUCUMBER (finely-chopped)
1 Tbsp. CHIVES (finely-chopped)
¼ cup HALF-AND-HALF
½ cup PECANS (chopped)
1 clove GARLIC (minced)
¼ tsp. ground BLACK PEPPER

1) Cook chicken breasts in boiling water until thoroughly tender.
Remove meat from bones and put in bowl.

2) Cook macaroni in boiling water until tender. Do not overcook!
Drain water off macaroni and immediately add cream cheese. Stir
well until cream cheese blends into macaroni.

3) Add chicken meat, peas, cucumber, chives, half-and-half,
pecans and garlic to macaroni and cream cheese mixture. Stir well to
blend. Season to taste with black pepper.

Serve this dish cold (or at room temperature) with bread and butter and
white wine, or serve as a hot dish topped with croutons.

Crunchy Fried Chicken

2 lbs. CHICKEN THIGHS and LEGS
   (or your favorite chicken pieces)
1½ cups PECANS (finely chopped
   in food processor or blender)
1 cup FLOUR
1 cup CORNMEAL
2 tsp. SALT
2 tsp. BLACK PEPPER
2 tsp. CAYENNE PEPPER
4 EGGS
½ cup BUTTER
4 cups VEGETABLE OIL

1) Cut up chicken into pieces, wash well and dry slightly.

2) Combine all dry ingredients in a bowl and mix well.

3) In another bowl, mix eggs and melted butter. Dip chicken pieces into the liquid mixture, then toss in dry mixture to coat thoroughly. Repeat this step for thick-coated chicken.

4) Heat vegetable oil in a large, deep skillet and add chicken pieces a few at a time. Fry about 10-12 minutes on each side. Drain on paper towels or a rack. Chicken may be refrigerated and used when desired.

Stuffed Turkey Breasts
with Orange Sauce

2 lbs. TURKEY BREAST CUTLETS
10 oz. CHICKEN BROTH (or bouillon)
¾ tsp. dried ROSEMARY (crushed)
2 Tbsp. GREEN ONIONS (thinly sliced)
¼ tsp. SALT
4 Tbsp. FLOUR
4 Tbsp. FROZEN ORANGE JUICE
**   CONCENTRATE (melted to liquid)**
2 ripe AVOCADOS (pitted/peeled)
1/3 cup PECANS (finely-chopped)
½ tsp. PEPPER

Pound turkey cutlets with meat mallet to about ¼-inch thickness. Coat cutlets lightly with about 3 Tbsp. flour. Set aside while preparing filling and sauce.

FILLING: Mash avocado meat and mix in pecans, salt and pepper. Roll about 1 Tbsp. of filling into each cutlet and secure with toothpicks. Place in shallow pan.

SAUCE: Blend remaining Tbsp. of flour into chicken broth. Add orange juice concentrate, rosemary and green onions. Cook over low heat, stirring constantly, until sauce is slightly thickened. Pour over stuffed turkey cutlets in pan.

Bake prepared dish in 350 degree oven for 50-60 minutes or until turkey meat is cooked through. Serve immediately. Makes about 8 servings.

Pecan Sweet Potato Puff

½ cup MILK
¼ cup BUTTER
4 cups (about two 1-lb. cans) SWEET
  POTATOES (mashed)
4 EGG YOLKS
1 cup PECANS (chopped)
½ cup SUGAR
¼ cup SHERRY
1 Tbsp. ORANGE RIND (grated)
¾ tsp. SALT
½ tsp. NUTMEG
4 EGG WHITES

Combine milk and butter; place over low heat until butter melts. Add to sweet potatoes slowly, beating constantly. Beat in egg yolks one at a time. Add pecans, sugar, sherry, orange rind, salt and nutmeg; mix well. Beat egg whites until they will hold soft peaks; fold into sweet potato mixture. Pour into 2-quart casserole or souffle dish. Bake in hot oven (400 degrees) until done, about 50 minutes. A knife inserted in center of the souffle will come out clean when done. Serve immediately. Yields 8 servings.

Pecan Pork Chop Casserole

6 PORK LOIN CHOPS (cut ½-inch thick)
1 cup CELERY (sliced)
1 Tbsp. COOKING OIL
1 cup dry ONION-MUSHROOM RICE MIX*
2 cups WATER
½ cup PECANS (chopped)
2 Tbsp. SOY SAUCE
PAPRIKA

Trim excess fat from chops and set aside. In saucepan, cook celery in oil until tender. Stir in rice mix and water. Bring to boil. Remove from heat; stir in nuts. Turn mixture into a 9x13x2-inch baking dish. Arrange chops atop rice. Brush chops with soy sauce, sprinkle with paprika. Bake, covered, in 350 degree oven for 25 minutes. Uncover and bake 10 minutes more, or until chops and rice are tender. Makes 6 servings.

*Rice mix: 3 cups LONG GRAIN RICE
1 envelope regular ONION-MUSHROOM SOUP MIX
¼ cup dried PARSLEY FLAKES
2 tsp. crushed dried BASIL

Vegetarian Loaf

1 cup BREAD CRUMBS
1 cup whole MILK
2 EGGS (well-beaten)
1 cup CARROTS (cooked and diced)
1 cup PEAS (cooked)
½ cup ONION (finely-chopped)
1 cup PECANS (finely-chopped)
½ tsp. POULTRY SEASONING
1 tsp. SALT
1 cup fresh MUSHROOMS (sliced)
¾ cup BUTTER
½ tsp. BLACK PEPPER

Soak bread crumbs in milk. Then add eggs, carrots, peas, onion and pecans. Season with poultry seasoning and salt; shape into loaf or place in casserole dish. Bake at 350 degrees for 45 minutes. Heat mushrooms in peppered butter. Pour over cooked loaf before serving. Makes 6 servings.

Lone Star Lamb Chops

6 LAMB CHOPS (cut to 1½-inch thick)
1 cup dry RED WINE
½ cup ORANGE JUICE
1 Tbsp. CHILI POWDER
¼ cup cooked GREEN CHILES (diced)
1/3 cup PECANS (chopped)
2 Tbsp. OLIVE OIL
1 med. ONION (chopped)
2 cloves GARLIC (minced)
1 tsp. GROUND CUMIN
1 tsp. SALT

1) Place lamb chops in deep baking dish. Combine all other ingredients and mix well. Pour mixture over lamb and marinate 24 hours in refrigerator, turning chops occasionally.

2) To cook, place lamb in roasting pan. Save marinade. Place lamb in oven preheated to 450 degrees. Cook 15 minutes, then reduce heat to 350 degrees, and pour marinade over meat. Cook at 350 degrees for 45 to 50 minutes or until meat tests tender.

Pecaned Picante Pasta

1 2/3 cups fresh SPINACH LEAVES (firmly-packed)
1 cup PICANTE SAUCE
2/3 cup PARMESAN CHEESE (grated)
½ cup PECANS (chopped)
1/3 cup OLIVE OIL
1 clove GARLIC (minced)
1 lb. LINGUINE (or other pasta of your choice)

1) Combine spinach, one-half of picante sauce, cheese, pecans, oil and garlic in a blender and mix on low setting until smooth. (A hand beater may be used if the spinach leaves are first chopped finely.) Set this mixture aside in a small bowl and stir in remaining picante sauce.

2) Cook pasta according to package directions until tender (do not overcook). Drain pasta and divide portions onto plates. Pour generous helpings of spinach mixture over pasta immediately. Sprinkle with additional chopped pecans and serve with a bowl of picante sauce on the table.

An excellent vegetarian dish which makes about 4 to 6 servings.

Cheesey Broccoli Casserole

1 lb. BROCCOLI (fresh)
1 can (10¾ oz.) CREAM OF CHICKEN SOUP
½ cup MILK
¼ lb. CHEDDAR CHEESE (grated)
1 cup PECANS (chopped)
½ cup BREAD CRUMBS

Cook broccoli in salted water until just tender. Drain and place in a greased 1-quart casserole. Add cheese and pecans. Mix soup and milk and pour over. Top with bread crumbs and bake at 350 degrees for 30 minutes.

Asparagus & Mushroom Casserole

1 can (15 oz.) ASPARAGUS (drained)
1 can (4 oz.) MUSHROOMS (drained)
3 EGGS (sliced, hard-cooked)
¼ cup PECANS (chopped)
1 can (10¾ oz.) CREAM OF MUSHROOM SOUP
3 oz. CHEESE CRACKERS (crushed)

Arrange ingredients in layers in greased casserole, reserving some of the crushed cheese crackers for the top. Bake at 350 degrees for 30 minutes. Yields 6 servings.

Chinese Mystery Loaf

1 ONION (chopped)
½ cup PECANS (finely-chopped)
½ cup BEAN SPROUTS (chopped or whole)
1 tsp. SOY SAUCE
¼ tsp. PAPRIKA
1½ tsp. LEMON JUICE
1½ cups COTTAGE CHEESE

Combine above ingredients and blend with cottage cheese until desired consistency is achieved. Pack firmly into loaf pan and chill in refrigerator. Cut into slices and serve.

Spiced Sweet Potatoes

4 medium SWEET POTATOES (about 2 lbs.)
¼ cup BUTTER
¼ cup BROWN SUGAR (firmly packed)
½ tsp. NUTMEG
½ cup PINEAPPLE (crushed)
¼ cup PECANS (chopped)
PECAN HALVES

Cook unpeeled whole sweet potatoes in boiling water until tender. Remove skins and mash until fluffy. Add other ingredients. Pour into 1-quart buttered casserole. Bake in 400 degree oven for 20 minutes. Garnish with pecan halves. Serves 6.

Vegetable Rice with Pecans

2 Tbsp. BUTTER
1 cup RICE (raw)
½ tsp. SALT
2 cups CHICKEN BROTH (hot)
½ cup PARSLEY (chopped)
½ cup CARROTS (chopped)
½ cup GREEN ONIONS (sliced)
½ cup CELERY (chopped)
½ cup PECANS (chopped)

Brown rice in butter and salt; pour into a casserole. Stir in broth. Cover and bake 45 minutes at 350 degrees. Add remaining ingredients and toss lightly. Bake 10 additional minutes. Yields 6 servings.

PIES

PIES

If you are starting with shelled pecans, you will find that the basic pecan pie is one of the simplest pies to make. Accidentally leave out one of the ingredients, however, and you'll discover that even though the ingredients are few, each has a definite purpose.

You'll find recipes for several types of pecan pies here. You may wish to keep in mind the following notes as you modify recipes to create a pie uniquely suited to your taste.

PECANS—They give a toasty crunchy topping, which is what this pie is all about. The amount can vary from one cup to two without altering the other filling ingredients. Chopped or in halves, just be sure the nuts taste fresh, not old and rancid.

EGGS—Usually three for the average pie, eggs provide the foundation for pecan pie's custard-like texture. Slightly beating the eggs results in an even distribution throughout the filling. Overbeating makes foam which rises to the top of the pie during baking and coats the nuts with a sugary crust.

If made with two eggs, the pie might come close to boiling over and has an unpleasant uneven texture. Four eggs gives a firmer pie and five tends to make the filling curdle. Substituting egg whites or egg substitutes for whole eggs causes the filling to foam and boil over.

SUGAR—A cup of sugar per pie is a good rule-of-thumb, although the sugar can be reduced to half a cup for a less sweet pie. Granulated white, light brown, or dark brown sugar can be used interchangeably with some variation in results. For example, the brown sugar may cause some slight weeping.

CORN SYRUP—Gives pecan pie its characteristic translucent look. A cup is generally used, and it matters not whether it is light or dark corn syrup. The dark variety will, however, give a darker color to the filling. Some cooks will use light corn syrup with granulated sugar for a pie with the lightest color and flavor and a satiny smooth filling. Dark brown sugar with dark corn syrup yields a dark pie with a flavor similar to molasses.

BUTTER or MARGARINE—Adds richness and flavor to the custard filling. Any amount from a tablespoon to half a cup works but the larger amount makes a softer filling.

VANILLA—A teaspoon or so of real vanilla is the traditional flavoring in a pecan pie, but other choices can include brandy, rum, almond, orange, and some spices such as cinnamon, nutmeg and cardamon.

Basic Pecan Pie*

4 Tbsp. (½ stick) BUTTER (softened)
1 cup granulated SUGAR
3 EGGS (slightly beaten)
1 cup light CORN SYRUP
1 tsp. VANILLA
⅛ tsp. SALT
1 cup PECANS (chopped)
9-inch PASTRY SHELL (unbaked)
PECAN halves

Cream butter and sugar together. Add remaining ingredients. Pour into unbaked 9-inch pastry shell. Top with 30-50 pecan halves. Bake 10 minutes at 375 degrees and 30-35 minutes at 325 degrees.

*Cooks who want to be exotic can add::
—**cream** (¼ cup) for a richer-tasting, less sweet custard.
—**liquor** (up to 2 Tbsp.) without affecting the consistency of the pie (larger amounts can cause curdling and a softer filling).
—**chocolate** (up to four 1-oz. squares or a 6-oz. pkg. of morsels) melted with the butter.
—**cocoa** (up to 1/3 cup) to the corn syrup for a fudge-like pie filling.

Millionaire's Pecan Pie*

1 can (14 oz.) SWEETENED CONDENSED MILK
2 cups pure MAPLE SYRUP
1 cup PECANS (chopped)
9-inch PASTRY SHELL (baked)

Mix all ingredients in sauce pan and bring to a boil while stirring occasionally to keep from sticking. Boil for four to seven minutes, depending upon your altitude. Pour into standard 9-inch baked pie shell. Cool. Top with whipped cream just before serving.

*This is the richest (and most expensive!) pecan pie recipe of which I am aware. And yet, it is so simple! Buy maple syrup in bulk from a food cooperative or natural foods store to save money. It will run about $2.50 per pound (depending upon the grade you buy) which is about half the cost of commercially-bottled maple syrup.

All-Natural Pecan Pie

9-inch PASTRY SHELL (unbaked)
2 cups whole PECANS
2 Tbsp. KUZU* (see note)
1 tsp. AGAR-AGAR POWDER
½ tsp. SEA SALT
1¼ cups WATER
2 Tbsp. CORN OIL
1 cup BARLEY MALT
¼ cup pure unrefined MAPLE SYRUP
2 tsp. pure VANILLA extract

Preheat oven to 350 degrees. Prepare your favorite 9-inch pie crust. Before baking the pie crust, layer the pecans on the bottom. Then bake on the lower shelf for about 25 minutes, until the pecans are toasted and crust is a light golden brown, but not done. Remove from oven and set aside; leave oven on.

While pie crust is baking, put the kuzu, agar-agar and salt in a saucepan. Add the water slowly in order to completely dissolve the kuzu. Then add the oil, barley malt, and maple syrup and blend thoroughly. Bring to a boil, stirring often. Reduce heat and simmer for 5 minutes; stir occasionally. Turn off flame; stir in vanilla. Slowly pour filling into pie shell; adjust the few pecans that have moved so they are evenly distributed. Return pie to lower shelf and bake 15 more minutes, making sure the crust doesn't get overdone. Remove from oven and set aside to cool for two hours. Then refrigerate for two hours or until filling sets. Serve warm or at room temperature.

*Some items may be available only at health food stores. **Kuzu,** also known as kudzu, is usually in chunky pieces, therefore, it is best to pulverize approximately what you'll need with a small mortar and pestle, or crush with a rolling pin and then measure the exact amount needed. The sweetness of this recipe can be adjusted to suit your own taste.

Cheesey Pecan Pie*

1½ cups GRAHAM CRACKER CRUMBS
½ cup (1 stick) BUTTER (softened)
1/3 cup PECANS (chopped)
2 pkgs. (8 oz. each) CREAM CHEESE (softened)
1 cup SUGAR
¾ cup PECANS (coarsely-chopped)
1 cup SOUR CREAM
2 Tbsp. SUGAR
2 tsp. VANILLA
PECAN HALVES

Combine graham cracker crumbs, butter and the 1/3 cup pecans in a small bowl. Mix well until crumbs form. Reserve 2 Tbsp. crumbs for top. Press crumbs onto bottom and sides of a 9 x 1½-inch pie plate. Chill for 20 minutes.

Beat cream cheese in a medium-size bowl with electric mixer until fluffy. Beat in the one cup sugar until mixture is smooth. Stir in the ¾ cup pecans; spoon into prepared crust.

Bake in a slow oven (325 degrees) for 20 minutes. Remove from oven to wire rack. Increase oven temperature to 350 degrees.

Blend sour cream, the remaining 2 Tbsp. sugar and the vanilla in a small bowl. Spread mixture evenly over baked filling. Return to oven.

Bake in a moderate oven (350 degrees) for 10 minutes. Garnish with pecan halves and reserved crumbs. Chill until firm, about three hours.

*This National Pecan Festival Cooking Sweepstakes recipe takes a bit of effort, but it is worth it!

Brown Sugar Pumpkin-Pecan Pie

1/4 cup PECANS (coarsely-chopped)
1/4 cup CANDIED ORANGE RIND or CITRON
   (moderately coarsely-chopped)
3 EGGS (lightly beaten)
1 can (1 lb.) PUMPKIN
2/3 cup LIGHT BROWN SUGAR (firmly packed)
1 tsp. ground CINNAMON
1/2 tsp. ground NUTMEG
1/2 tsp. ground ALLSPICE
1 cup EVAPORATED MILK
9-inch PASTRY SHELL (unbaked)

Scatter pecans and chopped orange rind over the bottom of an unbaked 9-inch pastry shell. Beat eggs lightly in large bowl. Stir in pumpkin, sugar, cinnamon, nutmeg, allspice and milk. Pour into pastry shell.

Bake in a hot oven (425 degrees) for 15 minutes, then lower temperature to moderate (350) and bake for 25 minutes or until filling is set. Cool pie to room temperature before serving. Garnish, if you wish, with fluffs of 1/2 cup heavy cream, whipped, and scatterings of 2 Tbsp. finely-chopped pecans and 2 Tbsp. finely-chopped candied orange rind. Makes 8 servings.

9-inch Pastry Shell

1 1/2 cups FLOUR (sifted)
1/2 tsp. SALT
1/2 cup SHORTENING
4 Tbsp. COLD MILK (or water)

Resift flour with salt into mixing bowl. Cut in shortening with pastry blender (or 2 knives) til size of peas. Sprinkle milk or water, tablespoon at a time, over dry ingredients, and gently toss with a fork. Mix lightly til all flour is moistened. (If necessary, add 1 or 2 teaspoons extra liquid.) Gather dough together and gently shape into ball. Roll out on floured cloth covered board to 10-inch circle. Roll from center to outside evenly in all directions. Lift rolling pin at edge of dough to keep edges from becoming too thin. Fold dough in half and lift into pie pan. Unfold and ease dough gently into place to fit pan. Build up a shallow fluted edge on pie rim.

Moo-Moo Pecan Pie

½ cup SUGAR
¼ tsp. SALT
2½ Tbsp. CORNSTARCH
1 Tbsp. FLOUR
3 cups MILK
3 EGG YOLKS (slightly-beaten)
1 Tbsp. BUTTER
1½ tsp. VANILLA
½ cup PECANS (chopped)
9-inch PASTRY SHELL (baked)

In a sauce pan, combine sugar, salt, cornstarch and flour; blend well. Gradually add milk, stirring to combine. Add slightly-beaten egg yolks and butter. Cook over medium heat, stirring constantly until mixture comes to a full boil. Cool slightly, add vanilla and pecans. Pour into baked pie shell* and cover with meringue. Bake at 400 degrees until delicately brown (about 8-10 minutes). Cool away from drafts. Refrigerate until serving time.

*Note to remember: of course, making homemade pie crusts takes time and a bit of skill. But, if you have a runny pie, it is usually caused by a refrigerated crust or frozen pie shell.

Honey Pecan Pie

½ cup HONEY
½ cup BROWN SUGAR
¼ cup BUTTER
3 EGGS (beaten)
1 cup PECANS
9-inch PASTRY SHELL (unbaked)

Blend honey and sugar together. Cook slowly to form a smooth syrup. Add butter. Add beaten eggs and pecans. Pour into pastry shell. Bake in 400 degree oven for 8-10 minutes. Reduce oven heat to 350 degrees and bake for 30 minutes, or until knife comes out clean.

Quick Chocolate Pecan Pie

1 lb. MILK CHOCOLATE*
1 container (8 or 9 oz.) WHIPPED TOPPING
9-inch PASTRY SHELL (baked)
1 cup PECANS (chopped)

Melt chocolate (with a little water added) in a double boiler. Fold in about ¾ of the whipped topping with the melted chocolate and put in a baked pastry shell while warm. Sprinkle with pecans. Refrigerate for 1-2 hours before serving.

Optional: An additional chocolate layer—perhaps of the semi-sweet variety—can be placed on the pie, and this can be capped with pecan halves.

*The more pennies you are willing to invest in the quality of your milk chocolate, the better tasting this recipe becomes. Giant Hershey's bars work fine, but try some imported variety some time.

Mock Pecan Pie

2 EGGS
½ cup BROWN SUGAR (firmly-packed)
½ cup DARK CORN SYRUP
½ cup (1 stick) melted BUTTER
1 tsp. VANILLA
¼ tsp. SALT
2/3 cup OATMEAL (quick-cooking)
9-inch PASTRY SHELL (unbaked)

Preheat oven to 350 degrees. Beat the two eggs slightly. Add to the eggs and mix until well blended the sugar, corn syrup, butter, vanilla and salt. Stir in oatmeal. Pour into 9-inch unbaked pastry shell. Bake 25-30 minutes, or until crust is golden brown.*

*Yields 10 slices at about 238 calories per slice. No pecans here, but this pie is certain to be a conversation starter!

Chocolate Pecan Pie

2 squares (1 oz. each)
    UNSWEETENED CHOCOLATE
3 Tbsp. BUTTER
1 cup LIGHT CORN SYRUP
¾ cup SUGAR
3 EGGS (slightly-beaten)
½ tsp. SALT
1 tsp. VANILLA
1 cup PECANS (chopped)
9-inch PASTRY SHELL (unbaked)

Preheat oven to 375 degrees. Melt chocolate and butter in double boiler. Combine corn syrup and sugar; simmer two minutes in separate pan. Add chocolate mixture to syrup mixture and cool. Add salt to slightly beaten eggs. Use pan large enough to add syrup mixture to eggs, slowly stirring constantly. Blend in vanilla and chopped pecans. Pour into unbaked pastry shell and bake for 35 minutes. Optional: top pie with whole pecans before cooking, if desired.

Golden Pecan Pie

3 EGGS
1 cup dark CORN SYRUP
1 cup SUGAR
2 Tbsp. BUTTER (melted)
1 cup PECANS (whole)
⅛ tsp. SALT
1 tsp. VANILLA
9-inch PASTRY SHELL (unbaked)

Mix corn syrup, sugar and butter with eggs. Add pecans, salt and vanilla, and stir to blend. Pour into unbaked pastry shell. Bake in 400 degree oven 15 minutes; reduce heat to 350 degrees and bake another 25 to 30 minutes. (Filling will be slightly less set in center than around edge.)

BAKED TREATS

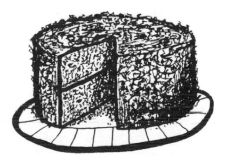

Pecan Rolls

1 pkg. DRY YEAST
¼ cup WARM WATER
¼ cup SHORTENING
¼ cup SUGAR
1 EGG
½ tsp. SALT
½ cup MILK (scalded)
2 Tbsp. ORANGE JUICE
3¼ cups FLOUR
2/3 cup PINEAPPLE (or apricot) JAM

Combine water and yeast in bowl. Add shortening, sugar, egg, salt and milk. Blend. Add juice and ½ flour. Knead well. Add remaining flour. Knead well again. Let rise until double, about 45 minutes. Punch down and let rest for 15 minutes. Roll dough into 10x18-inch rectangle. Brush with melted butter. Add jam and roll. Cut into 10 or 12 pieces and place on top of glaze.

GLAZE:

¼ cup BUTTER
1 cup BROWN SUGAR (firmly-packed)
1 Tbsp. WATER
1 tsp. LEMON (or orange) EXTRACT
1 cup PECANS (chopped-fine)

Place the first four ingredients in a skillet and heat slowly to boiling. When mixture begins to boil, count time and boil one minute without stirring. Put into 8x8x2-inch pan. Spread nuts evenly over mixture. Place segments of sliced dough face down on this mixture and bake at 375 degrees for 35-40 minutes. Let cool slightly and remove with spatula. Flip rolls over onto cool plate so glaze and nuts are on top.

Pecan Brownies

2 EGGS
1 cup SUGAR
2 squares (1 oz. each) unsweetened CHOCOLATE
1 tsp. VANILLA
½ cup all-purpose FLOUR (sifted)
¼ tsp. SALT
½ tsp. BAKING POWDER
½ cup BUTTER (melted)
1 cup PECANS (chopped)

Heat oven to 350 degrees. Beat eggs in medium-sized bowl until very thick. Gradually add sugar. Stir in melted chocolate and vanilla. Sift flour, salt and baking powder into the creamed mixture, and blend well. Add melted butter and chopped pecans. Spread batter in greased baking dish (8x8x2 inches). Bake 25 to 30 minutes. Remove from oven, cut in pan into 16 two-inch squares. Remove squares immediately. When cool, top with chocolate icing (below).

ICING:

1-lb. box POWDERED SUGAR
½ stick (¼ cup) BUTTER
Dash SALT
2 heaping tsp. COCOA
1 tsp. VANILLA
CHOCOLATE MILK

Mix all ingredients thoroughly, adding enough chocolate milk to get a spreading consistency. Spread icing over brownies and decorate each with a pecan half if desired.

Favorite Pecan Bars*

1 1/3 cups FLOUR
½ tsp. BAKING POWDER
1/3 cup BUTTER (softened)
½ cup BROWN SUGAR (firmly-packed)
¼ cup PECANS (chopped fine)

Sift together flour and baking powder. Add butter and sugar and mix until all particles are fine. Stir in pecans. Mix well. Pat into bottom of well-greased 9x13-inch pan. Bake at 350 degrees for 10 minutes, remove and cool.

PECAN TOPPING

2 EGGS
¾ cup dark CORN SYRUP
¼ cup BROWN SUGAR (firmly-packed)
3 Tbsp. FLOUR
½ tsp. SALT
2 tsp. VANILLA
¾ cup PECANS (coarsely-chopped)
30 PECANS HALVES

Beat eggs until foamy. Add corn syrup, brown sugar, flour, salt and vanilla. Mix thoroughly. Pour over partially-baked crust. Sprinkle with chopped pecans. Or, if desired, mix chopped pecans into filling and arrange pecan halves over top (one for each bar). Bake at 350 degrees for 25-30 minutes and let cool in pan. Cut into about 48 bars (about 1½ inch x 1½ inch). Place a pecan half on top of each bar.

*This is my favorite pecan recipe. I use Mexican vanilla (without added alcohol) and piloncillo, a Mexican brown sugar, to add a special flavor. Makes about 2½ dozen bars.

Old-Fashioned Filled Coffee Cake

1 pkg. DRY YEAST
¼ cup WARM WATER
1 tsp. SUGAR
1 cup BUTTER (melted)
1 cup HALF-AND-HALF (scalded, cooled)
4 EGG YOLKS (slightly-beaten)
3 Tbsp. SUGAR
1 tsp. SALT
4 cups FLOUR

Dissolve yeast in water. Add one teaspoon sugar. Combine butter, half-and-half, egg yolks, three tablespoons sugar and salt in large bowl. Mix well. Add yeast and water. Stir. Add flour gradually. Beat thoroughly. Cover and store in refrigerator overnight. Divide dough into three equal portions. Roll each piece into a 16x12-inch rectangle.

NUT FILLING:

1½ lb. PECANS (ground)
1 cup SUGAR
4 EGG WHITES (stiffly-beaten)
Grated RIND of 2 LEMONS

Mix pecans, sugar, egg whites and rind well. Spread 1/3 of filling on each rectangle. Roll from narrow side. Place rolls side by side in a buttered 15x10x1-inch pan. Cover and let rise for about two hours. Bake at 350 degrees for about 45 minutes.

German Chocolate Cake

1 pkg. (4 oz.) German sweet CHOCOLATE
½ cup BOILING WATER
1 cup BUTTER
2 cups SUGAR
4 EGG YOLKS
1 tsp. VANILLA
2½ cups FLOUR
½ tsp. SALT
1 tsp. BAKING SODA
1 cup BUTTERMILK
4 EGG WHITES (stiffly-beaten)

Melt chocolate in boiling water and cool. Cream butter and sugar until fluffy. Add egg yolks, one at a time, beating well after each. Blend in vanilla and chocolate. Sift flour with soda and salt; add alternately with buttermilk to chocolate mixture, beating after each addition until smooth. Fold in beaten whites. Pour into three 8- or 9 inch layer pans. Bake at 350 degrees for 35 minutes. Cool and frost with coconut-pecan frosting.

COCONUT-PECAN FROSTING:

1 cup EVAPORATED MILK
1 cup SUGAR
3 EGG YOLKS (slightly-beaten)
½ cup BUTTER
1 tsp. VANILLA
1½ cups COCONUT
1 cup PECANS (chopped)

Combine milk, sugar, egg yolks, butter and vanilla. Cook and stir over medium heat until thickened (about 15 minutes). Do not boil. Remove from heat and add coconut and pecans. Spread mixture over cake at room temperature.

Mazanek
(Bohemian Easter Bread)

2 cakes compressed YEAST (or equivalent yeast)
1 tsp. SUGAR
2 Tbsp. FLOUR
¼ cup MILK (lukewarm)
½ cup plus 2 Tbsp. BUTTER
1/3 cup plus 2 Tbsp. SUGAR
1 tsp. SALT
1 tsp. LEMON RIND (grated)
3 EGGS (slightly-beaten)
4¼ cups FLOUR (sifted)
¾ cup MILK (scalded)
¼ cup CITRON (thinly-sliced or chopped)
2/3 cup PECANS (chopped)
½ cup CURRANTS (or raisins)

1) Crumble yeast in a small bowl. Add one teaspoon sugar and stir until yeast is dissolved. Add 2 tablespoons flour and ¼ cup lukewarm milk (which has been scalded and cooled). Blend to a batter and let stand until bubbly.

2) Melt butter and stir in sugar until dissolved. Add salt, lemon rind and slightly-beaten eggs. Blend this into yeast mixture. Gradually add sifted flour and remaining milk, and beat until smooth and elastic.

3) Add citron, pecans and currants or raisins, and blend well.

4) Place in lightly-greased bowl. Brush top with melted butter. Cover and let rise in warm place (about 2 hours).

5) Turn out onto lightly-floured board and work into a smooth round ball. Place on greased cookie sheet. Let rise to double size (about 45 minutes).

6) Cut a cross in the center of top using a sharp knife. Do not cut too deeply into the dough.

7) Gently brush top of dough with slightly-beaten egg white. Sprinkle a few finely chopped pecans over the top. Bake in a 375 degree oven 40 to 50 minutes or until bread tests done. Remove to cake rack and cool.

OPTIONS:
A) Sprinkle bread with sifted powdered sugar.
B) While still warm, brush with icing of your choice. (If loaf is to be glazed with icing, omit brushing top of dough with egg whites. Also hold chopped pecans for sprinkling after icing is applied.)

Lover's Choice*

FOR CAKE:

1 pkg. (18½ oz.) YELLOW CAKE MIX
½ cup SALAD OIL
4 EGGS
1 can (11 oz.) MANDARIN ORANGES (undrained)
½ cup PECANS (finely-chopped)

Combine cake mix, oil, eggs, nuts and mandarin oranges (including juice). Beat with a mixer for two minutes. Spoon into three greased and floured 9-inch round cake pans. Bake at 325 degrees for 25 to 30 minutes or until cake tests done. Cool in pans for 10 minutes. Remove from pans and cool completely on wire racks. When cake has cooled, spread frosting very thickly between layers. Stack layers, and use toothpicks or wooden skewers to hold layers atop each other (they will have a tendency to slide). Spread remaining frosting on top and sides of cake. Store in refrigerator for 15 minutes to allow frosting to firm slightly. Arrange pecan halves on top of cake. Stand pecans on edges around edge of cake for spectacular appearance.

PINEAPPLE-CHEESECAKE FROSTING:

1 can (20 oz.) crushed PINEAPPLE (undrained)
1 Tbsp. SUGAR
1 pkg. (10½ oz.) Jell-O CHEESECAKE MIX
  (don't use the graham cracker crust portion)
1 pkg. (8 oz.) SOUR CREAM
1 container (9 oz.) frozen WHIPPED TOPPING
½ cup PECAN HALVES

Combine pineapple, sugar, cheesecake mix and sour cream. Stir until mixture thickens. Fold in whipped cream.

*This is a very rich dessert. I make the frosting first and set it aside, because it must be allowed to firm up a bit before it can be easily handled as a frosting. Even then, you will find that this cake greatly improves with age. By the second and third day in the refrigerator, cake has mellowed into a delicious treat. With careful use of the pecan halves, you can make a beautiful dessert which you can prepare well ahead of time.

Pecan Logs

1 1/3 cups FLOUR (unsifted)
¾ cup BUTTER (softened)
1½ cups PECANS (finely-chopped)
3 Tbsp. SUGAR
¼ tsp. SALT
1½ tsp. VANILLA EXTRACT
¾ cup POWDERED SUGAR
¼ cup unsweetened COCOA

1) In large bowl, combine all ingredients except powdered sugar and cocoa. With hands, mix until thoroughly blended. Refrigerate 30 minutes. In a small plastic bag, combine ¼ cup powdered sugar and the cocoa; place remaining powdered sugar in another bag.

2) Preheat oven to 350 degrees. On pastry cloth sprinkled lightly with flour, roll out dough one-half at a time, ¼-inch thick. Cut into 3x½-inch strips. Place one-inch apart on ungreased cookie sheets.

3) Bake 8 to 10 minutes, or until cookies are set but not brown. Remove to wire rack; let stand one minute before removing from cookie sheets. Cool slightly.

4) Roll half in powdered sugar and half in cocoa mixture while still warm; cool completely. Just before serving, sprinkle with more sugar or cocoa mixture, if desired. Makes about 5 dozen.

Buttermilk Apple-Pecan Muffins*

1½ cups FLOUR
1 Tbsp. BAKING POWDER
¼ cup SUGAR
½ tsp. SALT
¼ tsp. BAKING SODA
½ tsp. CINNAMON
¼ tsp. NUTMEG
¼ tsp. ALLSPICE (optional)
1½ cups RAISIN BRAN CEREAL
½ cup PECANS (chopped and toasted)
2 EGGS (well-beaten)
1 cup BUTTERMILK
¼ cup BUTTER (melted)
2 medium peeled & cored APPLES (grated)

1) Combine flour, baking powder, sugar, salt, soda and spices in a large mixing bowl. Add cereal and pecans. Stir well.

2) Blend eggs, buttermilk and butter together well. Make a depression in the flour mixture and add the buttermilk mixture all at once. Stir until the dry ingredients are moist. Fold in grated apples.

3) Fill muffin cups about ¾ full with batter. Bake at 425 degrees for 20 to 22 minutes, or until muffins are a light golden brown color. Serve immediately with butter, if desired.

*This recipe will make about 14 large muffins, each with about 170 calories and 1 gram of dietary fiber.

TIP: If you have no buttermilk, you can use milk with vinegar or lemon juice added (about 1 Tbsp. to 1 cup of milk). Let the milk and vinegar stand at least 5 minutes before using.

Chocolate-Pecan Meringue Cake

4 EGGS (separated)
½ tsp. CREAM OF TARTAR
1 cup SUGAR
1 pkg. DEVIL'S FOOD CAKE MIX
½ cup PECANS (chopped)
1 1/3 cups WATER
1/3 cup VEGETABLE OIL
1½ cups WHIPPING CREAM (chilled)
3 Tbsp. BROWN SUGAR
1½ tsp. VANILLA
WHOLE PECANS

1) Heat oven to 350 degrees. Grease and flour two round cake pans, 9x1½-inches. Beat egg whites and cream of tartar in small bowl until foamy. Beat in one cup sugar, one tablespoon at a time; continue beating until stiff and glossy. Do not underbeat.

2) Beat cake mix (dry), egg yolks, chopped pecans, water and oil in large bowl on low speed, scraping bowl constantly, until moistened. Beat on medium speed, scraping bowl frequently, two minutes. Pour batter into pans. Spread half of the meringue over batter in each pan to within ¼-inch of edge. Bake until meringue is light brown (about 40 minutes). (Meringue will crack.) Cool 10 minutes. Carefully remove from pans; cool cake completely.

3) Beat whipping cream, three tablespoons sugar and the vanilla in chilled small bowl until stiff. Fill layers with half of the whipped cream and brown sugar mixture; spread remaining amount over top. Garnish with whole pecans. Refrigerate at least four hours.

High altitude directions (3500 to 6500 feet): Heat oven to 375 degrees. Stir 2 Tbsp. all purpose flour into dry cake mix. Bake about 30 minutes. Carefully loosen meringue before removing from pan.

Pecan Sticks

PART 1:

> ½ cup SHORTENING
> 1½ cups FLOUR (sifted)
> ¼ tsp. SALT
> 1 Tbsp. SUGAR
> 1 EGG
> 2 Tbsp. WATER

Cream shortening and add mixture of flour, salt and sugar. Blend until mix is of coarse, even texture. Add egg and water. Stir to mix. Press dough evenly into greased 9x12-inch pan. Bake 20 minutes at 350 degrees.

PART 2:

> 2 EGGS (well-beaten)
> 1 cup BROWN SUGAR (firmly-packed)
> ½ tsp. SALT
> ½ tsp. BAKING POWDER
> 2 Tbsp. FLOUR
> ½ tsp. VANILLA
> 1 cup PECANS (chopped)

Add brown sugar to beaten eggs, then add combined salt, baking powder and flour. Beat until smooth. Add vanilla and pecans. Spread on pastry. Bake about 30 minutes. Cool and cut into sticks.

Elf Treats*

DOUGH FOR THE CRUSTS:

½ cup FLOUR (unsifted)
¼ cup (½ stick) BUTTER (softened)
½ pkg. (3 oz.) CREAM CHEESE

Preheat oven to 350 degrees. To make dough for the crusts, combine flour and ¼ cup butter. Mix with fork until the consistency of coarse meal. Add cream cheese, softened and cut into pieces. Continue to mix until dough is smooth. Form into a ball, wrap in plastic and refrigerate for at least one hour.

FILLING:

1 EGG
½ cup dark BROWN SUGAR (firmly-packed)
1 Tbsp. BUTTER (melted and cooled)
½ tsp. VANILLA
SALT
1/3 cup PECANS (finely-chopped)

To make filling, beat together egg, brown sugar, one tablespoon butter, vanilla, plus a pinch of salt. Divide dough into equal portions (12 for miniature tins, six for regular) and press evenly into the bottom and sides of ungreased muffin cups. Fill 1/3 of each cup with chopped pecans. Then spoon in enough filling to almost fill the cup (they'll puff up during baking and overflow if too full).

Top off with a pecan half on each and bake for 15 minutes or until filling begins to crack and is slightly firm to the touch.

"These miniature pies baked in muffin tins can be made in advance, thawed in the refrigerator, and served at room temperature accompanied, if you wish, by some rich vanilla ice cream.

Fancy Pecan Torte

2 cups PECANS (coarsely-chopped)
5 EGGS (separated)
1 cup SUGAR
2/3 cup BUTTER
1 tsp. VANILLA
½ cup ZWIEBACK TOAST crumbs
   (finely-crushed or ground)
POWDERED SUGAR
Whole PECANS
Sweetened WHIPPED CREAM (optional)

In a food processor or blender, whirl nuts until finely-ground like flour (watch closely; overprocessing may turn nuts into butter). Set aside.

In a large bowl of an electric mixer, beat egg whites at high speed until foamy. Then gradually beat in ½ cup of the sugar, one tablespoon at a time, until whites hold stiff, glossy peaks.

In another bowl, beat together butter and remaining ½ cup sugar until creamy. Beat in egg yolks and vanilla until fluffy. Mix in ground nuts and zwieback crumbs.

Gently stir in about 1/3 of the beaten whites to lighten mixture. Then gently fold in remaining whites until blended. Pour into a greased and floured 9-inch cheesecake pan with removable bottom or spring-released sides.

Bake in 350 degree oven until a wooden toothpick inserted in center comes out clean and top springs back when gently touched (45 to 55 minutes).

Let cool on a wire rack (cake will settle slightly). Remove pan sides. Lightly sift powdered sugar over top; garnish with whole pecans. Cut in wedges and offer with sweetened whipped cream, if desired. Makes 8 to 10 servings.

Honey-Nutty Tart

FILLING:

1 cup PECAN HALVES
2 cups additional NUTS (some combination of
   almonds, walnuts, filberts, macadamias
   and pistachios)
3 EGGS
1 cup HONEY
½ tsp. ORANGE PEEL (grated)
1 tsp. VANILLA
¼ cup BUTTER
Sweetened WHIPPED CREAM (optional)
BUTTER PASTRY*

Place any unroasted pecans and other nuts in a shallow pan and put into a 350 degree oven until lightly toasted (about 10 minutes); let cool. In a bowl, combine eggs, honey, orange peel, vanilla and melted butter; beat well until blended. Stir in toasted nuts. Pour into pastry-lined tart shell*. Bake on the bottom rack of a 350 degree oven until top is golden brown all over (about 40 minutes). Let cool on a wire rack. Remove pan sides. Offer wedges with whipped cream. Makes 10 to 12 servings.

BUTTER PASTRY:

1 1/3 cups FLOUR
3 Tbsp. SUGAR
½ cup BUTTER (cut into pieces)
1 EGG YOLK

Combine flour, sugar and butter. Whirl in a food processor or rub between your fingers until coarse crumbs form. Add egg yolk and stir until dough sticks together. Press evenly over bottom and sides of 11-inch tart pan with removable bottom.

Pecan Applesauce Cake

1¾ cup FLOUR (sifted)
1¼ tsp. BAKING POWDER
¼ tsp. BAKING SODA
½ tsp. SALT
¼ tsp. NUTMEG
½ tsp. CINNAMON
¼ tsp. GROUND CLOVES
½ cup BUTTER
1 cup SUGAR
1 EGG (well-beaten)
¾ cup strained, thick APPLESAUCE (unsweetened)
1 cup seedless RAISINS
1 cup PECANS (chopped)

1) Sift flour with baking powder, baking soda, salt and spices three times to ensure proper blend.

2) Cream butter and sugar together until light and fluffy. Add egg and beat well. Add flour mixture alternately with applesauce. Beat well, then add raisins and pecans.

3) Pour into well-greased loaf pan. Bake in moderate oven (350 degrees) for one hour and 10 minutes. Use a 9x5x3-inch pan. Turn out cooked cake onto rack to cool thoroughly. Frost top with an icing of your choice*.

*I frost this cake with a tart lemon icing, which is more lemony than sweet, to drizzle down the sides of the cake. To make icing, combine:

¼ cup LEMON JUICE
¼ cup HONEY
1 Tbsp. LEMON RIND (grated)
2 tsp. POWDERED SUGAR

Arrange pecan halves in icing for decoration.

Spicy Pecan Muffins

2 cups FLOUR
2/3 cup SUGAR
1 Tbsp. BAKING POWDER
½ tsp. SALT
1 tsp. CINNAMON
½ tsp. ground ALLSPICE
¼ tsp. ground CLOVES
1 EGG (slightly beaten)
1 cup MILK
4 Tbsp. BUTTER (melted)
1 cup fresh or frozen CRANBERRIES
   (coarsely-chopped)
½ cup PECANS (finely-chopped)

1) Preheat oven to 425 degrees. Thickly butter a 12-cup muffin tin. Combine flour, sugar, baking powder, salt and spices in mixing bowl, and stir until well blended. Make a well in the center. In separate bowl, combine egg, milk and butter, and blend thoroughly.

2) Pour egg, milk and butter mixture into dry ingredients and stir with wooden spoon just until ingredients are moistened. DO NOT OVERMIX!

3) Carefully fold in cranberries and pecans. Spoon batter into muffin cups about half full. Bake 20 to 25 minutes until lightly browned. (Note: Muffins made with frozen berries take longer to bake.)

Jumbo Raisin-Pecan Cookies

2 cups RAISINS (seedless)
1½ cups WATER
1 cup (2 sticks) BUTTER
1 tsp. CINNAMON
¼ tsp. NUTMEG
¼ tsp. ALLSPICE
1 tsp. VANILLA
2 cups SUGAR
3 EGGS
4 cups FLOUR (sifted)
1 tsp. SALT
1 tsp. BAKING POWDER
1 tsp. BAKING SODA
1 cup PECANS (chopped)

Simmer seedless raisins in water. Drain and save ½ cup of the liquid. Blend shortening, cinnamon, nutmeg, allspice and vanilla. Gradually add sugar, creaming thoroughly. Beat in eggs, one at a time. Sift together flour, salt and baking powder. Add soda to the ½ cup of raisin liquid. Add flour mixture alternately with liquid to creamed mixture, stirring well. Add raisins and pecans. Chill. Drop by spoonsful on greased baking sheet. Bake in 400 degree oven 10 to 12 minutes. Makes 3 dozen.

Crowned Coffee Tarts

2 Tbsp. INSTANT COFFEE
¾ cup HOT WATER
¼ tsp. SALT
¼ cup SUGAR
3 EGG YOLKS (beaten)
1 envelope unflavored GELATIN
¼ cup COLD WATER
3 EGG WHITES (beaten)
¼ cup SUGAR
6 TART SHELLS
1 cup PECANS (halves)

Dissolve coffee in hot water in top of double boiler. Add salt and ¼ cup sugar. Cook over direct heat until sugar is dissolved. Slowly add hot liquid to egg yolks, stirring constantly; then return mixture to top of double boiler. Stirring, cook mixture until slightly thickened; remove from heat. To this, add gelatin which has been softened in cold water and stir until dissolved. Chill until consistency of unbeaten egg whites. Fold chilled mixture into stiffly-beaten egg whites to which remaining sugar has been added. Turn into 6 tart shells and garnish with whipped cream and pecans.

Pecan Pie Cookies

1 cup (2 sticks) BUTTER
½ cup SUGAR
½ cup dark CORN SYRUP
2 EGG YOLKS
2½ cups FLOUR
2 EGG WHITES

Cream butter and sugar. Add corn syrup and egg yolks. Beat until well blended and stir in flour. Chill several hours. Roll dough into 1-inch balls and brush with egg whites. Bake at 375 degrees for 5 minutes. Roll ½ tsp. chilled pecan filling* into ball and press into center of each cookie. Return to oven. Bake 5 minutes longer or until lightly browned. Cool 5 minutes and remove from cookie sheet.

*PECAN FILLING:

½ cup SUGAR
¼ cup BUTTER
3 Tbsp. dark CORN SYRUP
½ cup PECANS (chopped)

Combine sugar, corn syrup and butter in saucepan and cook, stirring occasionally until mixture boils. Remove from heat; stir in pecans. Chill.

Sunday Morning Coffee Cake

1 Tbsp. BUTTER (melted)
1 Tbsp. BROWN SUGAR
¼ tsp. CINNAMON
¼ cup CORN FLAKES (crushed)
½ cup PECANS (pieces)
1 cup FLOUR (sifted)
1½ tsp. BAKING POWDER
½ tsp. SALT
½ tsp. CINNAMON
¼ cup SUGAR
⅛ tsp. MACE
¼ cup SHORTENING
¼ cup seedless RAISINS (chopped)
1 EGG
¼ cup MILK

Prepare topping by mixing melted butter, sugar, cinnamon, corn flakes and pecans. Set aside. Preheat oven to 400 degrees. Sift together flour, baking powder, salt, sugar, cinnamon and mace. With pastry blender, work shortening into flour mixture and add raisins. Add egg, well-beaten, with milk, but do not overbeat. Pour into greased 6-inch pie tin, brush with melted butter and spread topping over it. Bake for about 30 minutes.

Danish Rum-Date-Nut Squares

COOKIE CRUST:

1¼ cups FLOUR
2 Tbsp. MAPLE SYRUP
1 stick BUTTER

Mix flour with syrup. Cut in butter until crumbly. Press into bottom of an 8- or 9-inch square baking pan. Bake at 400 degrees for 10-15 minutes or until golden brown. Set aside to cool.

TOPPING:

8 oz. CREAM CHEESE
1 cup DATES (pitted, chopped)
½ pint WHIPPING CREAM
1 tsp. VANILLA
½ tsp. ground CINNAMON
½ cup PECANS (chopped, roasted)
1 tsp. RUM FLAVORING

Blend softened cream cheese with dates and rum flavoring. Add vanilla and cinnamon. Whip cream until stiff peaks form. Fold this into the cream cheese mixture and stir in the pecans. Spread on cookie crust. Allow to cool and cut into squares.

No-Bake Fruitcake

1 lb. seedless RAISINS
1 lb. pitted DATES
1 lb. dried FIGS
1 lb. shredded COCONUT
½ lb. fresh CHERRIES (pitted)
1 lb. shelled PECANS
¼ tsp. SALT
1 tsp. VANILLA EXTRACT

1) Combine raisins, dates, figs, coconut, cherries and pecans in a suitable bowl. Mix well.

2) Chop mixture coarsely in a food processor or blender. Be careful not to overblend!

3) Empty mixture into a large mixing bowl. Add salt and vanilla. Blend well by hand.

4) Spoon and pack mixture into a mold or molds of your choice (or use two 6-cup loaf pans).

5) Cover (wrap) and place in a cold place to "age" for at least two days. Slice thinly when serving. Makes about five pounds.

Oasis Cake

1 cup FLOUR
1½ cups PECANS (chopped)
1 cup DATES (chopped)
1 cup SUGAR
3 EGGS (beaten)
½ tsp. BAKING POWDER

Mix half of flour with chopped pecans and chopped dates. Add remaining flour, sugar, beaten eggs and baking powder. Turn into single-layer greased pan. Bake in 275 degree oven about 45 minutes.

Pecan Bread Pudding

1 cup SUGAR
2 cups WATER
½ cup MOLASSES
1 tsp. CINNAMON
¼ tsp. CLOVES
6 slices BREAD (toasted)
1½ cups LONGHORN CHEESE (grated)
1 cup RAISINS
2 cups PECANS (chopped)

Combine sugar, water, molasses, cinnamon and cloves. Boil until sugar is dissolved. In a buttered casserole, layer bread, cheese, raisins and pecans. Pour hot syrup over ingredients. Bake at 350 degrees for 20-30 minutes, until syrup is absorbed.

Pecan Date Macaroons

4 EGG WHITES
1¼ cup fine SUGAR
½ lb. DATES (cut fine)
½ lb. PECANS (ground fine)
½ tsp. VANILLA

Beat egg whites stiff. Gradually add sugar. Beat until very thick and heavy. Add dates, pecans and vanilla. Mix lightly. Drop by teaspoonful onto a cookie sheet, buttered and floured. Bake at 350 degrees for about 20-25 minutes.

Greek Nut Cookies*

1 cup (2 sticks) BUTTER (softened)
¼ cup SUGAR
3 Tbsp. BRANDY
3 cups FLOUR (sifted)
2 cups PECANS (finely-chopped)
POWDERED SUGAR

1) Beat butter, sugar and brandy in a large bowl until smooth. Stir in flour to make a soft dough. Work in pecans until well-blended.

2) Shape dough by tablespoonsful into balls. Place one inch apart on ungreased cookie sheet.

3) Bake in a slow oven (300 degrees) for 25 minutes or until bottoms are brown and tops are lightly golden. Remove from cookie sheet; roll in powdered sugar. Cool on wire racks. When cool, roll in sugar again. Store in tightly-covered containers.

*These buttery, melt-in-the-mouth confections can be frozen and stored.

Pecan Cocoons

1 cup PECANS (chopped)
2¼ cups FLOUR
5 Tbsp. POWDERED SUGAR
¾ cup BUTTER

Chop pecans and mix with flour and powdered sugar. Melt butter and add to dry ingredients. Roll the dough into cocoons the size and shape of your thumb. Bake in slow oven (250 degrees) about 45 minutes.

Buttermilk Pecan Loaf

4 cups FLOUR
1 tsp. BAKING SODA
1½ tsp. BAKING POWDER
½ tsp. SALT
2 EGGS
2 cups BROWN SUGAR (firmly-packed)
3 Tbsp. BUTTER
2 cups BUTTERMILK
2 cups PECANS (chopped)

Preheat oven to 350 degrees. Sift together flour, baking soda, baking powder and salt. To well-beaten eggs, gradually add sugar and beat well. Blend this with melted butter. Then combine flour mixture and buttermilk alternatively with egg mixture, stirring well. Mix in chopped pecans. Bake in two greased loaf pans in 350 degree oven for about one hour.

Quick Pecan Cookies

½ cup (1 stick) BUTTER
1½ cups BROWN SUGAR
1 EGG
1½ cups FLOUR
1 tsp. VANILLA
1 cup PECAN HALVES

Cream butter with brown sugar and egg. Add flour, vanilla and pecan halves. Shape into little balls, place on buttered cookie sheet and flatten out to ⅛-inch thick rounds. Bake about 12 minutes in 375 degree oven until nicely browned. Makes 3 dozen.

In-a-Hurry Pecan Sugar Cookies

2 Tbsp. BUTTER
½ cup SUGAR
1 EGG
½ tsp. VANILLA
¾ cup FLOUR (sifted)
⅛ tsp. SALT
1 tsp. BAKING POWDER
2 Tbsp. MILK
¾ cup PECANS (chopped)

Cream butter and sugar together. Add egg and beat well. Add vanilla. Sift flour, salt and baking powder into the creamed mixture, and add the milk. Fold in pecans. Drop by teaspoonsful two inches apart on greased cookie sheet. Decorate cookies with pecan halves. Bake in 400 degree oven 5 to 8 minutes. Makes 3 dozen cookies.

Chocolate Pecan Dollars

½ cup BUTTER
1 cup SUGAR
1 EGG
2 Tbsp. MILK
2 tsp. VANILLA
2¼ cups FLOUR
1 tsp. BAKING POWDER
½ tsp. CINNAMON
1 cup PECANS (chopped)
2 squares (1 oz. each) semi-sweet CHOCOLATE

Cream butter and sugar. Add egg, milk and vanilla. Add flour, baking powder, cinnamon, sifted together. Mix. Add pecan pieces and melted chocolate. Form into rolls 2 inches in diameter. Wrap in waxed paper. Use a sharp knife to cut into ⅛-inch slices. Remove wax paper and place discs on a slightly greased cookie sheet. Bake at 375 degrees for 8-10 minutes.

Pecan Pound Cake

1 lb. (4 sticks) BUTTER
1 lb. POWDERED SUGAR
2 cups EGGS (8 to 10 medium or large)
1 Tbsp. BRANDY (or vanilla)
½ tsp. NUTMEG
¼ tsp. MACE
4 cups FLOUR (sifted)
1 cup PECANS (chopped)

Preheat oven to 350 degrees. Generously grease the bottom of a 10-inch tube pan or bundt pan. In a small skillet, saute pecans in two tablespoons of the butter until lightly browned. Set aside to cool while mixing cake. Cream butter until fluffy. Add sugar and beat until very well blended. Add flavoring and spices and mix again. Add flour gradually and beat until light and well-mixed. Fold in the chopped pecans. Pour into cake pan and bake for one to 1¼ hours or until an inserted toothpick comes out clean.

Bull's Eye Cookies

½ cup (1 stick) BUTTER
¼ cup BROWN SUGAR
1 EGG YOLK
1 cup FLOUR (sifted)
1 EGG WHITE
1 cup PECANS (finely-chopped)
JELLY

Cream butter with sugar. Beat egg yolk until light and add to butter-sugar mixture. Blend in flour. Form into balls the size of your thumb. Dip in slightly-beaten egg white. Roll in chopped pecans. Place on greased cookie sheet. Make a depression in center. Bake in moderate oven (350 degrees) for about 8 minutes. Remove from oven and press down centers again with finger. Continue baking 10 minutes longer. Cool slightly and fill centers with jelly of your choice.

Pecan Thins

½ cup BUTTER
1½ cups SUGAR
2 EGGS
3½ cups FLOUR (sifted)
2 tsp. BAKING POWDER
½ cup MILK
1 cup PECANS (chopped)
1 cup CITRON (chopped)
1 cup DATES (chopped)
½ tsp. CINNAMON
½ tsp. LEMON JUICE
POWDERED SUGAR

Mix all ingredients well together. Pat into 9x13-inch pan dusted with powdered sugar. Bake in 300 degree oven for 20-30 minutes (being careful not to overbake). Before removing from pan, cut into bars and sprinkle with more powderd sugar.

Crunchy Top Coffeecake

2 cups FLOUR (sifted)
1 cup SUGAR
1 Tbsp. BAKING POWDER
1 tsp. SALT
1 cup MILK
1/3 cup BUTTER (softened)
1 EGG
½ cup PECANS (chopped)
¼ cup SUGAR
1 tsp. CINNAMON

Sift flour, sugar, baking powder and salt into 3-quart bowl of electric mixer. Beat in milk, butter and egg at medium speed (2 minutes), scraping sides of bowl often. Pour into greased and floured 9-inch square pan. Combine pecans, sugar and cinnamon in bowl. Mix thoroughly and sprinkle over batter. Bake in 350 degree oven about 35 minutes (or til cake pulls away from sides of pan). Serve warm.

Pecan-Oatmeal Cookies

¾ cup FLOUR (sifted)
½ tsp. SALT
½ tsp. CINNAMON
¼ tsp. BAKING SODA
1 cup quick rolled OATS (uncooked)
1/3 cup SUGAR
1/3 cup BROWN SUGAR (firmly packed)
½ cup BUTTER (softened)
1 EGG
1 tsp. VANILLA
1 cup PECANS (chopped)
½ cup RAISINS

Sift flour, salt, cinnamon and baking soda onto waxed paper. Mix oats into dry ingredients. Beat sugar, brown sugar, butter, egg and vanilla in 1½-quart bowl til fluffy. Mix in dry ingredients. Stir in pecans and raisins. Drop with 2 teaspoons onto greased cooky sheet. Bake in center of 375 degree oven for 10 to 12 minutes. (Makes about 3 dozen cookies)

DESSERTS

Apple-Pecan Ice Cream

3 cups cooking APPLES (peeled, cored, coarsely-chopped)
¾ cup SUGAR
1 tsp. fresh LEMON JUICE
¼ tsp. CINNAMON
¼ tsp. NUTMEG
1 EGG
½ cup SUGAR
1½ cups MILK
1½ cups WHIPPING CREAM
½ tsp. VANILLA extract
⅛ tsp. SALT
¾ cup PECANS (chopped, salted)

1) Combine apples, ¾ cup sugar, lemon juice, cinnamon and nutmeg in a 3-quart saucepan with enough water to cover. Bring to boil, stirring frequently; reduce heat. Simmer, uncovered, until apples are soft. Remove from heat and let stand at room temperature until cool. Drain.

2) Place half of the apples in blender container; cover. Puree until smooth; repeat with remaining half of apples. Meanwhile, beat egg until foamy in large mixing bowl. Gradually add ½ cup sugar; beat until thickened. Add milk, cream, vanilla and salt. Blend in apple puree. Chill

3) Churn-freeze according to manufacturer's instructions for ice cream maker. Stir in pecans. After freezing, transfer ice cream to a plastic freezer container. Freeze ice cream 3-4 hours before serving. Yields 2 quarts.

Pecan Bavarian Cream

1 envelope (¼-oz.) UNFLAVORED GELATIN
1¼ cups COLD MILK
½ cup SUGAR
⅛ tsp. SALT
2 EGG YOLKS
½ cup PECANS (chopped)
½ tsp. VANILLA
1 cup HEAVY CREAM
2 EGG WHITES

In top of double boiler, soften one envelope gelatin with cold milk. Add sugar and salt. Stir until dissolved. Beat egg yolks slightly; pour small amount of hot mixture over yolks, then return this mixture to remainder in double boiler. Cook over hot water until mixture coats spoon. Chill until consistency of unbeaten egg whites. Stir in chopped pecans and vanilla. Fold gelatin mixture into cream (whipped). Then fold again into egg whites beaten stiff. Turn into mold and chill until firm. Unmold and garnish with whipped cream and pecan halves (if desired).

Crunchy Holiday Balls

1 lb. VANILLA WAFERS
1 cup PECANS (chopped)
2½ Tbsp. light CORN SYRUP
1½ Tbsp. COCOA
3 jiggers BRANDY (or ginger ale)
POWDERED SUGAR and CINNAMON

Crush vanilla wafers very fine. Add one cup chopped pecans, light corn syrup and cocoa. Add brandy or ginger ale, mixing well with finger tips. Roll into small balls the size of marbles. Roll in powdered sugar to which a small amount of cinnamon has been added.

Chocolate Fluff

7 EGG WHITES
¼ tsp. SALT
4 squares (1 oz. each) unsweetened CHOCOLATE
   (melted)
2/3 cup SUGAR
2/3 cup PECANS (chopped)

Beat egg whites with scant salt until very stiff. Gently fold in melted chocolate, sugar and chopped pecans. Turn into top of double boiler which has been well-greased and cook over hot water until souffle is firm in center (about 45 minutes). Serve immediately with whipped cream on hot plates.

Pecan Corn Fritters

2 EGGS
1 cup FLOUR
2 tsp. BAKING POWDER
1 can CREAMED CORN
¼ cup SUGAR
½ cup PECANS (finely-chopped)

Mix ingredients together and drop by spoonsful into hot oil. Cook until brown (about 5-7 minutes). Turn over to brown other side. Remove and set on paper towels. Sprinkle with powdered sugar. Makes about 30 fritters. Can be frozen.

Pecan & Fruit-Filled Cannoli Shells

12 oz. RICOTTA CHEESE
½ cup SUGAR
¼ cup flaked bitter-sweet CHOCOLATE
¼ cup PECANS (finely-chopped)
1 Tbsp. diced CANDIED FRUIT of your choice
1 Tbsp. Grande Marnier LIQUOR (optional)
3 Tbsp. HEAVY CREAM
CANNOLI SHELLS*

Mix ingredients together and cool. Fill cannoli shells and serve immediately.

*Filled cannoli shells are an excellent dessert accompaniment to pasta dishes. Cannoli shells can often be found on top of the cheese case at your grocers.

Recipe Notes

CANDY

Million Dollar Fudge

3 (4½-oz. each) CANDY BARS (plain chocolate)
2 pkgs. (6-oz. each) CHOCOLATE CHIPS
    (semi-sweet)
1 pint MARSHMALLOW CREME
1 Tbsp. BUTTER
1 tsp. VANILLA
4½ cups SUGAR
1 tall can (13-oz.) EVAPORATED MILK
1 lb. PECANS (chopped)

Mix chocolate candy bars (pieced), chocolate chips, marshmallow creme, butter and vanilla in 6-8-quart container. Set aside. Mix sugar and milk in 4-6-quart container and heat until mixture comes to a boil. Boil for 6 minutes. Pour into chocolate mixture, blending well. Add pecans and drop by tablespoons on waxed paper (or pour into well-buttered 9x12-inch pan). Let stand for six hours. Makes about six pounds.

Penuche*

4 cups BROWN SUGAR (firmly-packed)
½ cup MILK (or cream)
2 Tbsp. BUTTER
1 Tbsp. VINEGAR
1 cup PECANS (chopped)
1 tsp. VANILLA

Blend sugar, milk, butter and vinegar, and cook until a small amount will form a wax-like ball when dropped in cold water (soft-ball stage, 234 degrees). Remove from heat, add vanilla and nut-meats. Stir constantly until it hardens. Spread in buttered pans and cut into squares.

*Penuche is very similar in taste to pralines, though penuche is usually cut into squares. Of course, pecans can be substituted for peanuts in your favorite recipe for nut brittle.

Basic Pecan Pralines

4 cups SUGAR
1 tsp. SALT
2 cups CREAM (or evaporated milk)
3 cups PECAN HALVES

Mix three cups sugar, salt and cream together. Melt the other cup of sugar very slowly in a heavy skillet, stirring constantly until caramel-colored and syrup-like. Pour sugar and cream mixture into the syrup all at once and stir vigorously. Boil without stirring until syrup reaches soft-ball stage (234 degrees). Add pecans and stir well and quickly for several seconds. Drop by spoonsful on waxed paper to form flat, round patties.

Rich & Chewy Pecan Pralines*

2 cups SUGAR
2 cups light CORN SYRUP
1 lb. BUTTER
2 cups WHIPPING CREAM
2 tsp. VANILLA
7 cups PECANS (chopped)

Cook sugar and corn syrup together until candy thermometer reaches 245 degrees. Remove from heat and add butter. Stir until dissolved. Add 2 cups whipping cream slowly. Return to heat and cook until candy thermometer again reaches 245 degrees, stirring constantly. (This takes a while.) Add vanilla and pecans. Drop on foil that has been buttered. When cool, wrap in plastic. Makes about 80 pralines.

*This recipe was originally formulated by Mrs. Paul McComas, who used whole milk rather than whipping cream. This recipe is a bit richer and uses more nuts than the Basic Pecan Pralines or the Louisiana Cream Pralines.

Louisiana Cream Pralines

1 lb. light BROWN SUGAR
⅛ tsp. SALT
¾ cup EVAPORATED MILK
1 Tbsp. BUTTER
2 cups PECAN HALVES

Mix sugar, salt, evaporated milk and butter in a 2-quart saucepan. *
Cook and stir over low heat until sugar is dissolved. Add pecans and
cook over medium heat to soft-ball stage (234 degrees), stirring
constantly. Remove from heat and let cool five minutes. Stir rapidly
until mixture begins to thicken and coat pecans lightly. Drop rapidly
from a teaspoon onto aluminum foil or lightly buttered baking sheet
to form patties. (If candy becomes too stiff at the last to handle easily,
stir in a few drops of hot water.) Let stand until cool and set. Makes
about 44 small pralines.

*For variation, try adding 1½ teaspoons rum flavoring to sugar mixture
before cooking. Or add 1 teaspoon grated orange rind to sugar mixture
before cooking.

Pecan Caramels

1 cup WHITE SUGAR
½ cup BROWN SUGAR (firmly packed)
½ cup light CORN SYRUP
½ cup CREAM
1 cup MILK
¼ cup (½ stick) BUTTER
1 tsp. VANILLA
¾ cup PECANS (broken)

Combine sugars, corn syrup, cream, milk and butter, and stir over
low heat until the sugars dissolve. Continue stirring constantly over
increased heat until a small amount of mixture forms a caramel-like
ball in cold water. Remove from heat and add vanilla. Stir in broken
pecans and pour immediately into buttered loaf pan, to form a layer
about ¾-inch deep. When cool, remove from pan and cut into
squares with sharp knife dipped in hot water.

Pecan Divinity

2 1/3 cups SUGAR
2/3 cup light CORN SYRUP
½ cup WATER
2 EGG WHITES
¼ tsp. SALT
¾ cup PECANS (chopped)
1 tsp. VANILLA

Combine sugar, corn syrup and water in saucepan. Stir over low heat until sugar dissolves. When mixture boils, cover for one minute, then uncover and cook without stirring until a small amount dropped into cold water is brittle (265 degrees). When almost done, beat egg whites and salt on high speed until very stiff. Slowly pour the syrup in and continue to beat until no longer shiny and mixture will hold shape when dropped from a spoon. If too thick, stir in a few drops of boiling water. Add pecans and vanilla. Drop at once by teaspoonsful onto pan or turn into buttered pan to be cut into squares. Chopped candied cherries and chopped orange peel may also be added. Makes 4 dozen.

Apricot Balls

¾ cup dried APRICOTS
¾ cup flaked COCONUT
½ cup PECANS (chopped)
1 Tbsp. LEMON JUICE
½ tsp. LEMON RIND (grated)
½ tsp. ORANGE RIND (grated)

Wash and drain apricots. Add coconut and nuts. Put through a food grinder. Add lemon juice and lemon and orange rinds. Knead with the hands until well blended. Roll into small balls. If desired, the balls may be rolled in additional chopped nuts. Yields about 3 dozen balls.

Fondant*
(Uncooked with Pecans)

½ cup (1 stick) BUTTER
2 lbs. POWDERED SUGAR
1 can (14-oz.) SWEETENED CONDENSED MILK
1 Tbsp. VANILLA
2 cups PECANS (chopped)
1 pkg. (6-oz.) semi-sweet CHOCOLATE CHIPS
  (melted)

Mix butter, sugar, milk, vanilla and pecans thoroughly. Roll into small balls, chill 2 hours. Dip balls into melted chocolate. Place balls on waxed paper to cool.

*The name "fondant" comes from the French verb fondre, meaning "to melt." A word derived from the French for "sweet tooth" might better suit this candy!

Quick, No-Bake Rum Balls

½ lb. VANILLA WAFERS (ground or crushed)
1 cup POWDERED SUGAR
2 Tbsp. COCOA
1 cup PECANS (chopped)
½ cup light CORN SYRUP
¼ cup RUM

Combine dry ingredients; add nuts, syrup and rum. Stir until stiff. Coat hands with powdered sugar and roll mixture into balls of desired size. Let stand for about an hour on waxed paper, then roll in additional powdered sugar. Makes about 40.

Pecan Roll

2 cups WHITE SUGAR
1 cup BROWN SUGAR, firmly-packed
1 cup EVAPORATED MILK
¼ cup CORN SYRUP
Dash of SALT
½ pkg. (8 oz.) CARAMELS (melted)
PECANS (finely-chopped)

Butter sides of large saucepan before cooking. Blend the sugars, milk, corn syrup and salt, and cook to soft-ball stage (234 degrees). Cool to lukewarm. Beat until mixture can be handled, then knead until it will form a roll. Turn mixed roll into melted caramels, covering well, and then roll in pecans. Wrap in waxed paper to cool.

Chocolate Pecan Puffs

3 squares (1 oz. each)
UNSWEETENED CHOCOLATE
1½ cups EVAPORATED MILK
¾ cup SUGAR
Miniature MARSHMALLOWS
1½ cups PECANS (chopped fine)

Melt unsweetened chocolate in double boiler. Stir in milk and sugar. Cook, stirring constantly until mixture thickens. Drop in marshmallows one at a time, then remove with toothpick when coated. Roll in finely-chopped pecans and let harden on waxed paper.

Equivalents

1 tablespoon cornstarch...2 tablespoons
flour (for thickening)

1 teaspoon baking powder...1/4 teaspoon
baking soda and 1/2 teaspoon
cream of tartar

1 cup milk...1/2 cup evaporated milk
and 1/2 cup water

1 cup milk...1/2 cup condensed milk and
1/2 cup water (omit sugar
in recipe)

1 cup milk...4 tablespoons powdered milk
and 1 cup water

1 cup sour milk...1 1/3 tablespoons vinegar
and enough sweet milk to fill
one cup (or 1 1/2 tablespoons
lemon juice)

1 square chocolate...1/4 cup cocoa

1 cup cake flour...1 cup sifted all-purpose
flour less 2 tablespoons

Weights and Measures

Dash or Pinch ... less than 1/8 teaspoon
3 measuring teaspoons ... 1 tablespoon
8 measuring tablespoons ... 1/2 cup
16 measuring tablespoons ... 1 cup

2 cups ... 1 pint
4 cups ... 1 quart
4 quarts ... 1 gallon

1/4 lb. butter (one stick) ... 1/2 cup
1/2 lb. butter (two sticks) ... 1 cup
1 lb. butter (four sticks) ... 2 cups
1 lb. granulated sugar ... 2 cups
1 lb. confectioners sugar ... 3 1/2 cups
1 lb. brown sugar (packed)... 2 1/4 cups
1 lemon ... 3 or 4 tablespoons lemon juice
1 orange ...6 to 8 tablespoons orange juice

MISCELLANY

Pecan Turkey Stuffing

12 cups fresh WHITE BREAD cubes
1½ cup PECANS (coarsely-chopped)
½ cup PARSLEY (chopped)
1 Tbsp. POULTRY SEASONING
2 tsp. SALT
½ tsp. PEPPER
½ cup BUTTER
3 cups CELERY (chopped)
1 cup ONION (chopped)

1) In large bowl, combine bread cubes, pecans, parsley, poultry seasoning, salt, pepper; toss to mix well.

2) In hot butter in medium skillet, saute celery and onion until golden—7 to 10 minutes.

3) Add to bread mixture; toss lightly until well mixed.

4) Use to fill prepared turkey. Makes 12 cups, enough to stuff a 16-lb. turkey, 16 servings.

Whole-wheat bread cubes may be substituted for the white bread cubes. Add a teaspoon of sage to the spices, if desired.

Pecan Rice Stuffing

1 cup BUTTER
1 cup ONION (chopped)
1 cup CELERY (chopped)
¼ cup PARSLEY (minced)
8 cups cooked RICE (cooked in chicken broth)
2 cups PECANS (chopped)
2 tsp. THYME
1½ tsp. SALT
1 tsp. CELERY SEED
1 tsp. SAGE
½ tsp. GROUND CLOVES
½ tsp. PEPPER
½ tsp. NUTMEG

Melt butter in a Dutch oven. Add onion, celery and parsley. Saute over low heat until tender, stirring constantly. Add cooked rice, pecans and seasonings. Toss together lightly. Makes enough stuffing for a 12-16-lb. turkey.

Sauce Verde

1 cup MAYONNAISE
¼ cup WATERCRESS LEAVES (chopped)
1 tsp. LEMON JUICE
¼ cup PECANS (finely-chopped)

Mix well. Refrigerate for one hour before serving over hot or cold fish.

Spiced Plum Jam with Pecans

6 cups (about 4 lbs.) fully-ripe Italian PRUNE PLUMS
(these are the smaller, softer violet-colored fruits)
½ cup WATER
8 cups SUGAR
½ tsp. GROUND CLOVES
½ tsp. CINNAMON
¼ tsp. ALLSPICE
1 cup PECANS (finely-chopped)
1 box (1¾ oz.) powdered FRUIT PECTIN

TO PREPARE FRUIT: Pit, but do not peel, the plums. Cut into small pieces and chop. Fruit should be very soft and juicy. Add ½ cup water to fruit in a heavy saucepan. Bring mixture to a boil and simmer, covered, for 5 minutes or until fruit and liquid form a puree. Add spices.

TO MAKE JAM: Mix fruit pectin and nuts into fruit in saucepan. Place over medium-high heat and stir until mixture comes to a full, hard boil. Immediately add sugar and stir. Bring to a full rolling boil and boil hard for 1½ minutes stirring constantly. Remove from heat and skim off foam with metal spoon. Ladle quickly into jars, filling to within ⅛-inch of top. Wipe tops and threads of jars with clean damp cloth. Cover with two-piece lids. Process in boiling water bath for 5 minutes, timing when water returns to boil. Cool, test for seal and store. Makes 11 cups or 11 glasses (8 fluid oz. each).

Natural Breakfast Nutriment

2 cups PECANS (chopped fine in blender)
1 Tbsp. WHEAT GERM
1 unpeeled APPLE (cored and diced)
1 BANANA (sliced)
1 unpeeled PEAR (cored and diced)
1 cup RAISINS, seedless
1 tsp. BROWN SUGAR
Reconstituted NONFAT DRY MILK SOLIDS

Combine all ingredients except milk. Moisten mixture with milk. Serve. Yields 4 to 6 servings.

Honey Pecan Butter

½ cup (1 stick) BUTTER (softened)
¼ cup HONEY
1/3 cup toasted PECANS (finely-chopped)

In a small bowl, beat butter until smooth and soft. Beat in the honey, then mix in pecans. Use immediately or keep refrigerated. Allow to soften before using. Makes about 1 cup.

Some Questions and Answers about Pecans

*All right, pecans taste good, but are they good for me?

According to Mae Martha Johnson, Extension Food and Nutrition Specialist, New Mexico State University:

Pecans are rich in nutrients. Ten large nuts (20 halves) yield approximately 100 calories. The fat in pecans has a high ratio of polyunsaturated to saturated fatty acids. The amount of fat (approximately 71 percent) makes the pecan an excellent source of energy.

Like other nuts and legumes, pecans furnish calcium, phosphorous, iron, potassium and magnesium. Since the amount of sodium in pecans is too low to measure, they can be used to add texture and flavor to foods for low-sodium diets.

Pecans are also a good source of the B vitamins (thiamin, riboflavin and niacin).

Pecans are 10.43 percent protein, 73.41 percent fat, 10.99 percent carbohydrate, 1.62 percent crude fiber and 1.50 percent ash. One cup of pecan halves equal about 715 calories, 10 grams protein, 74 grams fat and 15 grams carbohydrates.

Furthermore, nuts are a good energy food because their benefits are long-lasting.

*Sometimes during the year I can make a good buy on a large batch of pecans. How should I store them?

Unshelled pecans keep at room temperatures for about six months. In a refrigerator, they keep for one to three years. The shell further protects the meat from light, heat, moisture and exposure to air—factors which tend to cause rancidity in the shelled product.

Shelled pecans should never be stored at room temperature. They should be kept in a cool, dark, dry place or in the freezer. In a refrigerator (about 40 degrees F) or the freezer, they remain in good condition for a year.

Remember, however, nut meats can pick up odors and

flavors of other foods, so store them in tightly-covered containers. Finally, keep in mind unsalted nuts have longer storage life than do salted ones.

*It is cheaper for me to shell my own pecans, and what the heck, I'm willing to do a bit of work to save a few pennies. Any suggestions?

A little moisture in the pecan makes shelling easier and increases the number of perfect halves. (Newly-harvested nuts may contain enough moisture for easy shelling.) Add moisture in one of the following ways to nuts which have been stored for some time and are dry:

1) Soak overnight in cold water. Drain and dry with paper towels.

2) Cover with water and bring to a boil. Remove from heat and let stand five minutes. Drain and rinse with cold water. Dry with paper towels.

With either method, the shelled pecans may need to dry slightly to restore crispness. Be sure to discard any kernels that are moldy, shriveled or dry, as they may prove bitter or rancid.

*My recipe calls for a cup of shelled pecans. How many unshelled nuts will I need?

Following are general guidelines: 2½ pounds of pecans in-the-shell yield one pound shelled halves or about 4¼ cups. Chopped nuts and pieces measure about 3½ to 4 cups per pound.

*I'd like to make a few pies ahead of time for a party. Do they keep well in the refrigerator?

Pecan pie is always best when eaten the same day it is made. But, it keeps well for several days. To store, thoroughly cool the pie and cover with foil or plastic wrap. Keep up to two days at room temperature or up to a week in the refrigerator. Wrapped tightly in foil, pecan pies can be frozen up to three weeks before the nutty top loses its crispness.

*Where in the world is "the world's largest pecan"?

The city of Seguin, Texas, is the proud owner of the world's largest pecan and has it displayed in the center of town at the courthouse square. This giant oversized fruit of the state tree of Texas measures in at about three feet long.

The nut won't be made into pie soon. It's made of metal and plastic! To see the monument, take U.S. Highway 90A or State Highway 123 to Seguin (35 miles east of San Antonio, Texas).

*How did the term "pecan" originate?

"Pecan" is from the American Indian (Algonquian) word "pakan" meaning "a hard-shelled nut."

*Where may I write for further information on pecans?

Try writing your state extension director. Addresses can usually be found in a good almanac. Or, contact the Director of Information, Extension Service, U.S. Department of Agriculture, Washington, DC 20250. (On the local level, call your County Extension Agent, whose phone number is usually found under your county government listing.)

The Louisiana Pecan Festival

Pecan lovers by the thousands flock to Colfax, Louisiana, each year during harvest time (early November) to participate in one of the South's largest and most unique festivals: the Louisiana Pecan Festival.

Colfax is an historic town with a population of about 1700, located on the Red River (Route 8) about 20 miles northwest of Alexandria in Grant Parish.

Local organizers of this event, which begins with the blessing of the pecan crop, brace for between 60,000 and 70,000 visitors who enjoy a wide variety of festivities running Thursday through Saturday and culminating in a fireworks display on Saturday night.

The folks in this area of Louisiana take their partying seriously, as all schools in the parish are closed on Friday so that children can enjoy the activities this day. There's games for the kids, and plenty of gospel singing and country music throughout the festival. Other events include a turkey shoot, rodeo and trail rides, an 8K run and fun run.

Of course, much of the festival centers around edible delights. Judges pick winners of the pecan-cooking contest on Friday. The Country Store offers visitors plenty of homemade pies, cookies and other items in a small, old-fashioned atmosphere.

Here's where you can buy a sack of pecans for your own experimentation, as well as many other local products which you just can't find many places any more: cane syrup, filé powder, sugar cane, maple syrup, sweet potatoes and spices of all types. Don't forget to visit the famous Sausage House!

Saturday features a two-hour parade led by the Pecan Queen. Civic groups, school bands, politicians and the Pecanettes—a song-and dance group—join lots of others on the march through town.

Then the carnival opens, and three blocks of booths and stores along the railroad tracks downtown welcome visitors and locals with typical southern hospitality.

The festival has been held each year since 1969. Colfax citizens don't fuss much about "prettying" up their town for the onslaught. No need to. Southern charm—and the tall, graceful pecan trees everywhere—takes care of everything.

For more information, call (318) 627-5196, or write Louisiana Pecan Festival, Colfax, LA 71417.

Index

Meet the Author!

Mark Blazek is fascinated by two areas of human endeavor—food and writing.

In *Pecan-Lovers' Cook Book,* his first cook book, he presents nearly 150 recipes using the native American food—the pecan.

Blazek has had more than 400 articles published in a variety of national magazines, ranging from *Science Digest* to *Writer's Digest,* including *Grit, Western Boatman* and *Treasure.*

Among his articles are many on food trivia. He writes a column called "Field Tips" for *Western and Eastern Treasures Magazine,* in which he offers recipes for foods to take on camping trips and those to prepare in the field.

In addition to the *Pecan Lovers' Cook Book,* Blazek has written the *New Mexico Writer's Handbook* and *Where to Collect Fluorescent Minerals in the United States.*

Mark graduated from high school in Downers Grove, Illinois, then attended Illinois Benedictine College. When he moved to Socorro, he attended the New Mexico Institute of Mining and Technology, where he was selected for inclusion in *Who's Who in American Colleges and Universities.*

While at the institute, he worked as a proofreader, later becoming assistant editor for the twice-weekly *Socorro Defensor-Chieftain.*

While attending the University of New Mexico, he was managing editor of the *Daily Lobo,* the student newspaper, and edited software and technical publications for an Albuquerque publisher.

In Albuquerque, he was an instructor for The Learning Connection, teaching such classes as Writing for Publication, Basic English Skills and Advanced Writing Techniques.

Moving to Austin, Texas, he became a student intern, assisting the editor of *Medical Self-Care Magazine.* Presently, he is serving as Austin editor of the *Montrose Voice* of Houston. Blazek covers the state legislative sessions, represents the publication to Austin area businesses and organizations, and also handles delivery of the paper.

He is continuing his studies in journalism, sociology and political science at the University of Texas at Austin. A member of the Austin Writers' League, his interests include nature photography, contemporary events and racquetball.

When he is not studying, teaching, editing or writing, you will find Mark preparing dinner for friends in his Austin home.

(Author's photo on page 112)

ORDER BLANK

Golden West Publishers

4113 N. Longview Ave.   Phoenix, AZ 85014

Please ship the following books:

_____ Arizona Adventure ($5.00)

_____ Arizona Cook Book ($3.50)

_____ Arizona Hideaways ($4.50)

_____ Arizona Museums ($5.00)

_____ Arizona—Off the Beaten Path ($4.50)

_____ Arizona Outdoor Guide ($5.00)

_____ California Favorites Cook Book ($3.50)

_____ Chili-Lovers' Cook Book ($3.50)

_____ Citrus Recipes ($3.50)

_____ Cowboy Slang ($5.00)

_____ Explore Arizona ($5.00)

_____ Fools' Gold ($5.00)

_____ Ghost Towns in Arizona ($4.50)

_____ Phoenix Street Maps Book ($4.00)

_____ How to Succeed Selling Real Estate ($3.50)

_____ In Old Arizona ($5.00)

_____ Mexican Family Cook Book ($5.00)

_____ On the Arizona Road ($5.00)

_____ Pecan-Lovers' Cook Book ($5.00)

_____ Sphinx Ranch Date Cook Book ($5.00)

_____ Tucson Street Maps Book ($5.00)

Enclosed is $_____ (including $1 PER ORDER for postage and handling)

_____
(NAME)

_____
(ADDRESS)

_____
(CITY)   (STATE)   (ZIP)

Pecan Lovers' Cook Book

by Mark Blazek

This order blank may be photo-copied.

COOK BOOKS

MEXICAN
Family Favorites
COOK BOOK

More than 250 easy-to-follow home-style favorite family recipes for tacos, tamales, menudo, enchiladas, burros, salsas, frijoles, chile relleno, carne seca, guacamole and sweet treats! *Mexican Family Favorites Cook Book* by Maria Teresa Bermudez (144 pages)...$5.00

ARIZONA
COOK BOOK

A taste of the Old Southwest, from sizzling Indian fry bread to prickly pear marmalade, from sourdough biscuits to refried beans, from beef jerky to cactus candy.

Arizona Cook Book by Al and Mildred Fischer (144 pages)...$3.50. *More than 100,000 copies sold!*

CALIFORNIA
FAVORITES
COOK BOOK

Treat yourself to the California lifestyle with this cornucopia of 400 recipes for avocados, citrus, dates, figs, nuts, raisins, Spanish and Mexican dishes, wines, salads and seafoods. *California Favorites Cook Book* by Al and Mildred Fischer (144 pages)...$3.50

COOK BOOKS

CITRUS RECIPES from the Citrus Belt

Tempting recipes for luscious pies, dazzling desserts, sunshine salads, novelty meat and seafood dishes! Plus tangy thirst-quenchers with oranges, grapefruit, lemons, limes, tangerines, etc.

Citrus Recipes from the Citrus Belt by Al and Mildred Fischer (128 pages) . . . $3.50

Sphinx Ranch DATE RECIPES

Enjoy the versatility of dates in these tempting recipes for breads, puddings, cakes, candies, fruitcakes, waffles, pies and a myriad of other fantastic taste treats.

It's all in the *Sphinx Ranch Date Cook Book* by Rick Heetland (128 pages). . . $5.00

CHILI-LOVERS' COOK BOOK

Chili cookoff prize-winning recipes and regional favorites! The best of chili cookery, from mild to fiery, with and without beans. Plus a variety of taste-tempting foods made with chile peppers.

Chili-Lovers' Cook Book by Al and Mildred Fischer (128 pages) . . . $3.50. *More than 50,000 copies sold!*

Recipe Notes